Concepts in the Social Sciences

Series Editor: Frank Parkin

Published Titles

Concepts in the Social Sciences

Orientalism

Ziauddin Sardar

Open University Press
Buckingham · Philadelphia

For Merryl: Scholar, Adventurer, Friend

Open University Press
Celtic Court
22 Ballmoor
Buckingham
MK18 1XW

email: enquiries@openup.co.uk
world wide web: http://www.openup.co.uk

and 325 Chestnut Street
Philadelphia, PA 19106, USA

First published 1999

A catalogue record of this book is available from the British Library

ISBN 0 335 20206 3 (pbk)   0 335 20207 1 (hbk)

Library of Congress Cataloging-in-Publication Data
Sardar, Ziauddin.
    Orientalism / Ziauddin Sardar.
        p.   cm. — (Concepts in the social sciences)
    Includes bibliographical references and index.
    ISBN 0-335-20207-1 (hbk)   ISBN 0-335-20206-3 (pbk)
    1. Asia—Foreign public opinion. Western.   2. Middle East—Foreign
public opinion. Western.   3. Asia—Study and teaching.   4. Middle
East—Study and teaching.   5. Imperialism.   6. East and West.
I. Title. II. Series.
DS12.S28   1999
950—dc21
                                                    99-21097   CIP

Typeset by Type Study, Scarborough, North Yorkshire
Printed and bound in Great Britain by
Marston Book Services Limited, Oxford

Contents

Preface

The problem of Orientalism, what makes the dissection and display of its skeletal being a tricky matter, is the very fact of its existence. Because Orientalism exists we have a world where reality is differently perceived, expressed and experienced across a great divide of mutual misunderstanding. To discuss Orientalism one has to urge people to go beyond this misunderstanding and see what has been made invisible; to distinguish a different outline in a picture that has been distorted by centuries of myopic vision.

There is nothing about Orientalism that is neutral or objective. By definition it is a partial and partisan subject. No one comes to the subject without a background and baggage. The baggage for many consists of the assumption that, given its long history, somewhere within or about the subject there is real knowledge about the Orient; and that this knowledge can be used to develop an understanding of the cultures East of the West. The task of this book is to undermine this assumption, and show that, even though the project of Orientalism has way passed its 'sell by date', it is colonizing new territories. After retrenching itself in scholarship and literary imagination, Orientalism has moved on to conquer film, television and CD-ROMs. Nowadays, the subject of Orientalism is not limited to what is conventionally seen as the 'Orient' but also includes Europe, the home of its origins, itself.

While Orientalism is real, it is still, nevertheless, an artificial construction. It is entirely distinct and unattached to the East as understood within and by the East. There is no route map, no itinerary locked within the subject to bridge that divide. It is my thesis that the fact of Orientalism will always impede understanding between the East and the West. We need to begin again, from different premises, and find new bases for genuine encounters with the people, places, history, ideas and current existence that is to the East of the West. With so much scholarship, so many literary and imaginative texts, so much at stake within the entire enterprise of Orientalism, this is an uncomfortable, unwelcome and disquieting message. It strongly recalls the question posed by Alun Lewis's poem the 'Maratha Ghats', itself an interesting Orientalist text, written while he was serving as an airman in India during the Second World War:

> And did a thousand years go by in vain
> And does another thousand start again?

The answer to both questions is the obstacle course of writing a book on Orientalism. Yes, on both counts. A thousand years of Orientalism are quite vain as a solid basis for knowledge about the East; and another thousand years can either provide a continuation of the trajectory of non- and hostile encounter or mark a new departure. The hardest thing to write is an invitation to acknowledge how little we really know when confronted by as large a library as the works of Orientalism.

I would like to take this opportunity to thank my friend Merryl Davies who provided truly invaluable help and support in every stage of writing this book. Her vast knowledge of European and non-Western history, coupled with an almost instant recall, are a constant source of amazement for me. Thanks are also due to Steve Fuller, who first suggested that I write this book, Vinay Lal, who constantly discussed and debated many of the points raised here, and Juliet Steyn, Sean Cubitt and Sohail Inayatullah for their comments and criticisms. Finally, I am grateful to Gail Boxwell and Aoife Collins for their invaluable help in researching this book.

The Concept of Orientalism

The Orient, the land to the east of the West, is a realm of stories. Its actuality has always been encapsulated in forms of storytelling as fact, fiction and fable. It invites the imagination. So let us begin with a story. A French diplomat working in China meets and falls in love with the leading 'lady' of the Beijing Opera. The liaison ultimately causes the diplomat to be tried and convicted for spying. This is the basic narrative of David Cronenberg's powerful film, *M. Butterfly* (1993) based on a play by David Henry Hwang, who also wrote the screenplay. 'Inspired by a true story' *M. Butterfly* presents a complete discourse on Orientalism.

At the outset, Rene Gallimard is a rather lack-lustre minor bureaucrat at the French Embassy in Beijing, an accountant, a dedicated bean counter who is disliked by his colleagues. He is a grey man: the kind of boring, worthy and politely educated person one shies away from at parties. Hwang uses the 'love story' and the biography of Gallimard to spin out the major themes and essential characteristics of Orientalism. The story opens in China in 1964 covering the period up to the onset of the Cultural Revolution before switching to France in 1968, the year of the student revolution. It covers the period of the Vietnam War when France acted as the eyes and ears of America in China. This backdrop enables Hwang to demonstrate the practical application of Orientalism to politics; he is as accurate in identifying the pathology of Orientalism in the Western psyche as he is in deploying its *realpolitick*. The two are not different stories; they are essential combined elements in the whole narrative of Orientalism. The pathology of the Orientalist vision is based on two simultaneous desires: the personal quest of the Western male for Oriental mystery and sexuality and the collective goal to educate and control the Orient in political and economic terms. By including the references to the student rebellion of 1968, Hwang also includes the use of the Orient as a device for internal criticism and domestic demands for internal reform in the West – the student revolutionaries on the streets of Paris all wave Mao's *Little Red Book*. Orientalism thus serves as both the external individual and collective desire to possess the Orient and the internal desire to appropriate the Orient.

While Gallimard represents the West, Song Liling, the object of Gallimard's desire, is the Western representation of the Orient. Neither the West nor the Orient are monolithic entities; both are complex, ambiguous and heterogeneous. The Orient consisted – and consists – of the great civilizations to the East of the West: Islam, China, India and Japan. Not only could the West not deny them a history, an established place in the scheme of things, but it also had to recognize their power and wealth. And it was their intellectual and military power and economic and cultural wealth that gave rise to Orientalism. As such, Orientalism is geographically bound – it grew out of the fact that the powerful civilizations of the East were a lure to the desires of Western civilization; and the civilizations of the East did not immediately collapse at the onset of Western power. But the West itself was not always 'the West'. The notion of the West as a political entity dates back to the sixteenth century. Before that there was Christendom. And it is in the encounters of Christendom and its closest neighbour, Islam, that the origins of Orientalism, and much of its history, can be traced. While *M. Butterfly* deals with China and, indirectly, with Japan, the original site of Western desire was Islam. It was in its encounter with Islam that the West first developed its vision of the Orient as an unfathomable, exotic and erotic place where mysteries dwell and cruel and barbaric scenes are staged. The Crusades, for example, both initiated and perpetuated the representation of Muslims as evil and depraved, licentious and barbaric, ignorant and stupid, unclean and inferior, monstrous and ugly, fanatical and violent. For Christendom, Islam was the darker side of Europe. The Protestant Reformation and the rise of the Ottoman Empire led to the transformation of Christendom to 'the West'. In the seventeenth and eighteenth centuries, 'the West' was largely a geographical designation and was synonymous with 'Europe' and the 'Occident'. The term 'Europe' has a longer history going back to the ancient Greeks and Romans and had much wider currency.

> Only in the aftermath of the nineteenth-century colonial penetration of India, China, and the Middle East did 'the West' take on a more prominent political role, as the signifier of Europe's imperial project. It was at this time that it began to include the United States, previously referred to as the 'New World', and to merge with the concept of 'civilisation', the term coined by the Enlightenment philosophers to describe the aim of social evolution, which they identified with the processes and institutions marking the development of private property, the family, and monetary relations.[1]

Western civilization thus became the yardstick, as Christendom had been earlier, by which Oriental cultures and civilizations were measured. The conceptual category of 'the West' was pitted against the concept of the 'Orient' and the Orient came to signify all that the West was not and some of what the West actually desired.

In *M. Butterfly* the meeting of West and East begins at an Embassy reception. The evening's entertainment is a performance of the death scene from Puccini's *Madame Butterfly* by a local artiste, Song Liling. Gallimard admits he has never seen *Madame Butterfly* before. While other members of the audience note the local artiste does not have the voice for the role, Gallimard is entranced to the point of obsession. He approaches Song Liling; and their first conversation sets up the dynamic of the story:

> *Gallimard*: I have always seen opera singers as overweight ladies and too much bad makeup.
> *Song*: Bad makeup is not unique to the West.
> *Gallimard*: I've never seen a performance as convincing as yours.
> *Song*: Convincing? Me as a Japanese woman? Did you know that Japanese used thousands of our people for medical experiments during the war. But I gather such an irony is lost on you.
> *Gallimard*: No, what I meant was that you made me see the beauty of the story. Of her death. It's pure sacrifice. He is not worthy of it; but what can she do? She loves him so much. It's very beautiful.
> *Song*: Why yes! To a westerner.
> *Gallimard*: I beg your pardon.
> *Song*: It's one of your favorite fantasies. The submissive Oriental woman, the cruel white man.
> *Gallimard*: I don't think so.
> *Song*: Consider it this way. What would you say if a blond cheerleader

fell in love with a short Japanese businessman. He marries her then goes home for three years during which time she prays to his picture and turns down marriage from a young Kennedy and when she learns her husband has remarried she kills herself. Now I believe you would consider this girl to be a deranged idiot, correct? But because it is an Oriental woman who kills herself for a westerner you find it beautiful.

Now, most educated persons would know that the roles of women in traditional Chinese opera are played by men. It was also the European convention of Shakespeare and Molière. But Gallimard is determined to see Song not just as a woman but as a personification of a particular type of woman: 'the submissive Oriental woman'. Hwang is arguing that what is essential to the obsession of the Orientalist vision is the desire not to know. The object of love is not the physical person of Song Liling, either as man or a man playing the part of a woman. The object of love is Madame Butterfly, the operatic creation, whom Gallimard is determined to find in Song Liling. The supposed knowledge derived from the Orientalist vision is based not on accuracy and utility but by the degree to which it enhances the self-esteem of the Westerner. It achieves this by making fiction more real, more aesthetically pleasing than truth. Orientalism is thus a constructed ignorance, a deliberate self-deception, which is eventually projected on the Orient.

This fiction played a major role in Western scholarly tradition. The representations of cultures and civilizations to the East of the West that Orientalism came to signify were based on constructed ignorance – that is, they were deliberately concocted and manufactured as instruments to 'contain' and 'manage' these cultures and civilizations. As a scholarly tradition, Orientalism was concerned with the study of Asian civilizations, identifying, editing and interpreting the fundamental texts of these civilizations, and the transmission of this scholarly tradition from one generation to another through an established chain of teachers and students. It was largely focused on Islam; and Islamic studies became a major branch of Orientalism. Orientalism thus studied Islam and other civilizations with European ideas of God, man, nature, society, science and history and consistently found non-Western cultures and civilizations to be inferior and backward. It approached the Orient with specific notions of cultural history, the origins and development of religions, the ways in which sacred texts should be understood and interpreted, political ideas and how human societies evolve and develop. Orientalist scholarship was – is – the scholarship of the politics of desire: it codifies western desires into academic disciplines and then projects these desires onto its study of the Orient. It found Islamic, Chinese and Indian sciences, for example, to be not science and perpetuated the fiction that true science was created by and belonged to the West. Similarly, Islamic law was not law in any real sense; neither was Chinese medicine worthy of being referred to as medicine; and the Indian civilization had no notion of rationality – genuine reason was the sole privilege of Western civilization. On the ladder of evolution, the Orient was consistently way behind the West. Scholarly Orientalism became a highly fortified institution with its own apparatus – methods of teaching, communication network and a system for passing the 'torch' from teacher to student. It acquired its own style of thought and mode of analysis based on an ontological and epistemological distinction between the West and the Orient. It became a self-perpetuating and closed tradition which aggressively resisted all internal and external criticism; an authoritarian system that is flourishing as much today as it ever did in colonial times.

Hwang's main concern is to present a study of the psyche of Orientalism through what he takes to be its most significant ingredient, the allure of sex and the fiction of the submissive Oriental woman. His work takes its title from one of the great icons of this Orientalist vision, *Madame Butterfly*; the music and scenario of Puccini's opera runs throughout the film. Madame Butterfly ranks alongside Cleopatra and Mata Hari as personifications of the Orientalist complex, a pathology that finds fullest expression in real people who have literary lives. The interplay of reality with fiction is a central point, the point at which Orientalism attains its full being and potency. In his rendering of *M. Butterfly*, Hwang makes Rene Gallimard the iconic embodiment of the Orientalist, a neat parallel.

For Gallimard, *Madame Butterfly* is memorable for the beauty of its story, which is 'pure sacrifice'. As he develops this idea through the film he expands it to mean the unconditional love extended by Oriental women to men who are unworthy. This is an intoxicating idea for the West. After all, in one sense, it is the exact parallel of Christian theology. While Hwang appears not to be dealing with religion, *M. Butterfly* is an intrinsically religious text. Hwang subtly deploys essential Christian ideas to demonstrate their integral role

in the creation of the Orientalist vision. Pure sacrifice, unconditional love for the unworthy, these are familiar, indeed central
ideas within the constellation of Christianity. For Hwang, the fact
that the Western male is less besotted with the act of sex than the
idea of perfect love is somewhat akin to the passion of a celibate
divine. The sexual ambiguity is a major theme of the relationship
between Gallimard and Song Liling, whom he dubs 'my Butterfly'.
He finds Song Liling's manly body entrancing because it is like that
of a 'young girl', the paedophile complex being very near the
surface. But the sexual ingredient is much more ambiguous and
complicated. The love of children is also conceived as unconditional, and it gives the lover the added facility of being able to
mould, educate and inform. The paedophile impulse also adds a
new implication to Kipling's notion of the Other, that is the non-
west, as 'half devil and half child'. The Oriental women, in Gallimard's vision, offers all these charms, and much more. Orientalism
thus constructs the Orient as a passive, childlike entity that can be
lover and abused, shaped and contained, managed and consumed.

Gallimard's Butterfly offers him her shame, a modesty that maintains a mystique. When Gallimard first meets Song Liling at the
Beijing Opera 'she' is behind a gauze curtain, an image full of overtones of the harem and its hidden delights. While she is a virgin –
'though inexperienced I am not ignorant', Song tells Gallimard –
she has been schooled, as an Oriental woman, in exotic arts of love-
making and sexual pleasure-giving. Sexual pleasure within the
Western psyche is always associated with the notion of Original Sin,
within the Catholic psyche it retains the implication that the only
perfect life is the celibate life, sex always has the overtones of sin
and temptation. Sex then participates in the religious underpinnings of Orientalism. For the Western gaze, the Orient offers exotic,
sinful, sexual delights all wrapped in an ancient, mystical and mys-
terious tradition.

It is important to recognize that Gallimard comes to full possession of Orientalism through another allure, that of the ancient
culture and tradition of the Orient. 'His Butterfly' is a performer at
the Beijing Opera, a custodian of ancient culture and the home
where Gallimard visits 'her' is elegant and traditional. What Gallimard understands of his iconic Oriental woman is a function of her
embeddedness within ancient cultural tradition; it forms her character, gives her her knowledge. The façade Gallimard has created

egins.um theum

begins to crack with his first encounter with the Red Guards which culminates in their burning of the costumes of the Beijing Opera, recognized from the elaborate, delicate head-dress once worn by 'his Butterfly'. In the horror Gallimard experiences there is a strong implication of nostalgia for ancient tradition, a reminder that the West progresses and changes while the expectation is that the Orient remains unchanging in its adherence to tradition; and hence remains backward and buried in medieval history.

Orientalist scholarship had a particular stance on tradition. To begin with it emphasized ancient over living tradition. It discovered the 'past' of the Orient, a past over which it had more authority and control than the indigenous people. Islamic law, which has a long history and tradition, for example, was not merely studied by Orientalists, they actually constructed it. Legal Orientalism presented Islamic law in an essentialist manner and used this strategy to argue that Muslims are basically conservative tied to backward tradition and customs. In India, Orientalists did not only 'discover' the past, but constructed it in a specifically dualistic form: thus Muslims became foreigners who represented the inauthentic India while the authentic Hindus and their indigenous civilization had to suffer the oppression of the intruders. A new history was fabricated with a Hindu golden age which fell to the age of tyranny of Muslim invasions. When the British began to administer Bengal two of its officials could actually take this dualism to the limits of blindness. Asked to estimate the proportion of the Muslim, inauthentic population of Bengal, what is now Bangladesh, geographer James Rennell and former governor Henry Verdst both told a parliamentary committee that Muslims constituted only one-fifth of the population![2] Such historic and legalistic constructions were used to characterize Oriental societies as despotic by nature. Oriental despotism was a product of the absence of institutions of civil society without which it was not possible to break free from feudalism. Muslim societies, for example, had no independent cities or rational bureaucracy, or legal stability or an enterprising bourgeois class or the rights and freedoms that go with any legal and civic culture. There was thus a total absence of independent institutions to mediate between individuals and the state. Thus the individual was permanently exposed to the arbitrary rule of the despot. The absence of civic society not only promoted Oriental despotism, it also ensured that Muslim societies could not develop economically.

So, feudalism, despotism and economic backwardness were all intrinsic in the nature of Islam.

Gallimard's veneration of an idealized, iconic Oriental woman also invokes another characteristic of Orientalism – the white man as god syndrome. The white man as god is the teacher beloved, the most natural object of tuition to the unformed child who gives unconditional love and therefore reinforces the sense of self worth of the teacher. The white man mistaken for a god is one of the oldest clichés in contemporary books, cartoons and movies – think of the Rudyard Kipling story made into the John Huston film, *The Man Who Would Be King*; or the adventures of *Indiana Jones in the Temple of Doom*; or almost any adventure that sets off into Darkest Africa. These are not disinterested reports, or literary deceits, but consciously deployed ideology to explain the innate superiority of Europe to all parts of the European psyche. In pre-modern Orientalism, that is when the West was first engaging with the great civilizations of Islam and China, the white man as god is the missionary bringing the Christian message. In his encounter with Africa and the 'New World' of the Americas, the missionary is mistaken by simple, ignoble savages to be god. This myth is based on the legend that the Aztecs permitted a bedraggled band of Spaniards to penetrate to the heart of their empire because they believed them to be the white god which mythology foretold would come from the West. Exactly the same mythological trope is invoked to explain why Hawaiians first accepted and venerated Captain Cook as the god Lono, and then killed him in re-enactment of the ceremonial drama of the Lono myth. Peter Schaffer's play, and the movie thereof, *Royal Hunt of the Sun* uses this conventional European legend, this time concerning the arrival of the Spaniards in the Inca empire, and explores the complex attractions to European colonizers of being taken for gods by simple benighted savages.

In more modern times, the white man becomes the god of scientific wonder and superior technology. The bearers of such advancement must be a thing of wonder for the unsophisticated Other incapable of conceiving such refined marvels for themselves. As Gallimard notes, on a number of occasions in the opera, Madame Butterfly worships the picture of Pinkerton long after he had deserted her. The half child that comes complete with sexual temptation and allure, accoutred with exotic sexual licence, must in these Christian connections awaken the idea of the half devil. There is a further association to bear in mind. In medieval Western thought the East was the location of the Garden of Eden, so placed on all medieval maps. When Columbus first arrived in the Americas, thinking he had succeeded in reaching the East, the borders of Cathay (China), he identified the outflow of the Orinoco river as the mouth of the River of Paradise which flowed through the Garden of Eden. What else does one find in the Garden of Eden but an Eve ready to tempt man with forbidden knowledge? Hwang is subtly indicating the deep-rootedness of the Orientalist vision in the Western psyche. He is also indicating how it is constructed out of basic tenets of Western thought. Orientalism is not a construction from experience of the Orient. It is the fabulation of pre-existing Western ideas overwritten and imposed upon the Orient. The Orient, as exemplified by its iconic women, is submissive – the only proper response to a 'god'.

Once he has become aware of Madame Butterfly, Gallimard is lost in his obsession and pursues 'his Butterfly'. The important point is the effect on Gallimard of this new possession. The grey man becomes transformed. He looks, dresses and speaks with a new manner, he is promoted at work and placed in charge of intelligence. Most importantly he speaks with confidence and determination about the nature of China, its intentions and the *realpolitick* of East–West relations. The business side of Gallimard's life is an extension of his possession of a true Orientalist vision. Here the half devil/half child partakes of bigotry, racism and chauvinism in another seamless web. The man who possesses the idealized iconic Oriental women finds Orientals *en masse* unappealing as numerous script lines imply. But the most revealing point of knowledge in the world of *realpolitick* comes in the discussion of French colonial history in Indo-China. Gallimard must acquire information on behalf of the Americans who are fighting in Vietnam where France underwent the humiliation of Dien Bien Phu. 'Do you really think those little men could have beaten us without our unconscious consent?', he asks the French ambassador. The influence of the relationship with the Oriental woman underlies all of his political judgements. Again Gallimard tells the ambassador that the secret of China is that deep down it is attracted to Western ways, though it could never openly admit such an enormity. The child is ready to be tutored, the unconditional love for the person of an individual white man is itself an iconic representation of love of the West and all its ways. So China will eventually open itself to Western business. Further, submissiveness is not merely an aspect of the Oriental woman, it is an integral part of the Oriental character which will always submit to greater force. So for America to triumph in Vietnam it must show force and determination.

Power is an essential ingredient of Orientalism. For amongst the fascinations of the relationship with the iconic Oriental woman is the use of power to be cruel and inflict punishment. This is openly expressed: in their first intimate encounter, Song Liling accuses Gallimard of cruelty and reiterates the point in her letters to him. The Orient offers all the forbidden pleasures of sadomasochism, the pleasure that comes from giving pain. Gallimard enjoys referring to and thinking of 'his Butterfly' as a slave, a slave being one to whom one can be cruel, that one can punish with impunity and whose function by definition is to be humiliated. This is how imperial powers saw their subject people. Orientalism justified both the exploitation of Asian people and their political subjugation.

As counterpoint to Gallimard as the embodiment of Orientalism, Hwang presents Song Liling as far removed from Gallimard's fantasy. Fiction and ambiguity meet in an open discourse. Song Liling is no cipher, but a sentient character caught in the dynamics of his own real world where the fiction of Orientalism is able to serve both his own personal needs, to gain favour with the authorities, and where the very deception of the fiction enables Gallimard to be manipulated as a source of information useful to the Communist authorities. The information Song Liling extracts is precise and accurate, numbers of American troops to be deployed in Vietnam, in contrast to the flights of fancy Gallimard espouses as the fruits of his espionage. The themes of deception, truth and lies, fiction and knowledge, Hwang seems to argue, are central ingredients to the discourse of Orientalism.

The onset of the Cultural Revolution breaks Gallimard's world. In disgrace for his faulty intelligence he is sent home to France. Song Liling is sent to be re-educated as a bourgeois reactionary element after taking leave of Gallimard. Back in France, Gallimard attends a performance of *Madame Butterfly*. Even a heavy dose of reality fails to shatter his dream of the Orient. When Song Liling arrives in France she is able to convince Gallimard to participate in open espionage activities for China. He becomes a dispatch rider and hands over diplomatic pouches for inspection. Not surprisingly, he is caught and put on trial. The court asks Song Liling, who now appears in his real guise as a man, whether Gallimard was not aware of the deception. His reply is that he never asked and therefore does not know. As Song Liling and Gallimard are taken from the court in the same police van, Song Liling strips naked and offers himself to Gallimard. And Gallimard finally accepts the truth: 'How could you who understood me so well make such a mistake?', he says. 'You show me your true self. What I loved was the lie, the lovely lie'. Orientalism then is the great lie at the centre of the Western civilization: a lie about the nature of the West and about the nature of the great cultures and civilizations to the East of the West, a lie about Us and Them. As a corporate institution – that includes a tradition of scholarship, a framework of analysis expressed through theology, philosophy and sociology, techniques of representation, styles of fiction and travel writing, modes of expressing power and knowledge, and an elaborate system of accounting for differences – for managing and containing the Orient, Orientalism is sustained by a consuming love of 'the lovely lie'.

Imprisoned for treason, Gallimard prepares to perform the death scene from *Madame Butterfly* for the inmates. Conscious that to his fellow countrymen he is a joke, he tells his audience that men such as they should not laugh. The culmination of the film is Gallimard's monologue as he paints himself with stage makeup to become Madame Butterfly. It is Hwang's strongest assertion on the nature of Orientalism: Gallimard has become Orientalism. His final words are: 'My name is Rene Gallimard also known as Madame Butterfly'. The ultimate ambiguity is that the Orientalist is consumed by self-love. Orientalism is a creation of the Western psyche that unleashes power but at the end of the day its most important impact is not in the relations of power and dominance of the real world of politics, economic and military relations. Its greatest potency is within the psyche of the West itself where, as the perfect vision of perfect love, it has the greatest aesthetic power. To live without this vision is not just to lose control over the real world of politics, economic and military power, it is to lose part of the Western self. As Gallimard becomes a bizarre parody of a Japanese woman in a ridiculous wig, Puccini's music plays on. At the crucial moment Gallimard slits his own throat while the inmates of the prison applaud the secret he has shared with them. *M. Butterfly* comes to the chilling conclusion that the West would rather die than give up its Orientalist vision, even though it is a knowledgeably ignorant fiction, a fiction whose dissembling is known. The created vision of the Orient, Hwang argues, has become an integral part of the aesthetic of the West. In *M. Butterfly* the West chooses death rather than truth on aesthetic grounds. A world without the vision of Orient is too awful a place to contemplate.

A Short History

Orientalism has a long history, as befits a concept that partakes of the life force of Western self-identification. Conventionally its history is expressed as the emergence of a factual study through solid intellectual advance out of the errors of earlier credulity, ignorance and misunderstanding. Orientalism, in its modern guise, is the product of incremental, progressively more impartial, neutral, rational body of enquiry and learning. The most common allegation made in defence of Orientalism as a rational 'scientized' enquiry is that an object worthy of study, an object that is the Orient, actually exists. An examination of the history of Orientalism as it has actually operated shows this claim to be false, because its predication and assumptions turn out to be illusory. The history of Orientalism shows it is not an outward gaze of the West toward a fixed, definite object that is to the east, the Orient. Orientalism is a form of inward reflection, preoccupied with the intellectual concerns, problems, fears and desires of the West that are visited on a fabulated, constructed object by convention called the Orient. What that Orient is, is a shifting, ambiguous compendium, a thing that identifies whatever the writer, inscriber or supposed observer wishes it to mean or be at the moment. A real, as opposed to a pseudo, history of Orientalism must concern itself with the strands, trends and conventions that have gone into the construction of the movable feast that is the Orient constructed by Orientalists. A history of Orientalism is essentially a history of the ideas that have moved the West, most definitely it is not a history of the closer movement of the West to involvement with or understanding of the East, those details are incidentals. The Orient of Orientalists is a constructed artefact through which the West explains, expounds, objectifies and demonstrates its own contemporary concerns.

To indicate how history works within the conventions of Orientalism, let us look at two major examples of the genre, one from somewhere after the beginning, the other from only yesterday: *The Travels of Marco Polo*[1] and Wittfogel's *Oriental Despotism*.[2] Master Marco Polo's work was enormously popular and authoritative over a period of centuries. Its significance is said to be that it opened Cathay, China, to the Western imagination, placing its *il milione*, millions of stories, where virtually nothing had been previously known. What is known of the book itself is highly ambiguous, no actual original exists, every manuscript that does come down to us is different, containing interpolations, interpretations, mistakes and additions from the various copyists. Greatest ambiguity of all is the recent contention that Marco Polo may never have visited China at all.[3] As with so many early accounts of the Orient this is an irrelevance, myth is not important because it is myth, it is important because of what people do, and think and claim to know, in the name of reality that may be no more than myth. What spread all across Europe, and became a foundational part of the Western canon, is a rumbustuous book that in effect made the Orient a palace of Western desires. What we know of the writing of the book adds two further strands of importance. Marco Polo dictated his book to a hack ghost-writer, Rusticello, while both were prisoners of war. For Marco Polo the book seems to have been intended as a kind of résumé, a verification of his credentials to be a traveller-trader in the service of the high and the mighty. This purpose is effected by detailing the service he performed for the Great Cham, the Kublai Khan, who emerges in the book as the most all-powerful, richest and most revered emperor of them all. Kublai's empire is vast, populous and contains riches undreamed of in Europe. Indeed the East that Polo envisages gets all the best things of the world, only the leavings reach Europe. It is also barbarous and pagan, and therefore free of the conventional restrictions and prescriptions of the Christian world, so Polo tells of the sensual and exotic. The man who returns to report such a palace of desires must be fit to serve the economic, political and informational needs of his own society. A great deal of the form of the book is conventional, that is within literary conventions already well established in Europe. The style is the contribution of Rusticello, who is thought to be the same Rusticello who wrote Arthurian romances for the court of Prince Edward of England. In which case there is a salient parallel that needs to be made clear. Arthurian romances, at the period Rusticello would have been constructing them, were a means of appropriation by which the colonizing society of Norman England was taking over the literary traditions of its conquered Celtic marches, the place where the Arthurian tradition originates.[4] Rusticello then knew all about assimilating appropriated information into the conventions of dominance. So while the East is bigger, richer and better in some senses, it is also simultaneously remote, subservient and inferior. It is precisely this amalgam that guaranteed the longevity and centrality of the work over the centuries in preference to other reports of China that might be termed more rationalist and better written, yet which sank in the learned imagination almost without trace.

Karl August Wittfogel was almost unique in the annals of Orientalist system builders: he knew Chinese and was therefore able to examine his sources in their original, when writing of China, and he had actually been to China. His major work *Oriental Despotism*, originally published in 1957, was written after a lifetime of study that centred on China. However, to understand the text and thesis advanced by Wittfogel it is much more important to know his autobiography, it alone makes sense of the historical extent of his work and its preoccupations, expressed in his subtitle, 'A Study in Total Power'. Born in Germany, Wittfogel was the son of an Evangelical Lutheran schoolteacher. As a student he gravitated to the Separatist movement of Rosa Luxemburg and Karl Liebknecht. After their deaths in 1919 he became a member of the Communist Party. Wittfogel worked as a teacher, playwright and party activist while studying European economic history, Chinese history and language at the University of Frankfurt. His main interest was in Marx's concept of the Asiatic mode of production, he wanted to advance the study of this concept by synthesizing Marx and Weber. One of his friends in Communist circles was the playwright Bertolt Brecht. In 1931 Wittfogel chaired the discussion after a performance of Brecht's controversial play, *The Measures Taken*, about Russian Comintern revolutionaries in China, controversial for its somewhat heretic Marxist line. Wittfogel himself was considered something of a rebel, vehemently opposed to Nazism he disagreed with the Comintern's decision to avoid a direct conflict with the Nazis. As a result

he was excluded from major conferences on the Asiatic mode of
production held in Russia, despite being the acknowledged expert
on the subject. When the Nazis came to power in 1933, Wittfogel
was imprisoned in various SS camps for a year, before being
released thanks to international pressure from academics. He then
went to China and among other things learned a good deal about
the Chinese Communists, whom he tried to convince of the horrors
of the Stalinist purge trials, though he declined to meet Mao. When
the Japanese invaded China he made his way to the United States,
where he settled. He broke with the Communists completely on
learning of the Stalin–Hitler pact. After that he made a political
journey rightward, becoming increasingly suspicious of left-leaning
and liberal intellectuals, supporting the McCarthy hearings of the
1950s and becoming obsessive about the powers of totalitarianism;
therefore, *Oriental Despotism*, a study of continuous totalitarianism. The function of China's history, indeed of the history of all the
Orient, is to be the precursor of contemporary Communist totalitarianism that is with us still in Maoist China. Wittfogel is a traditional Orientalist also in constructing an Orient that is in effect 'the
Indies', that indeterminate usage ascribed to any space beyond
Europe that led Columbus to dub native Americans Indians, and
still has us calling the islands of the Caribbean the West Indies. He
includes in his study not only China but India, the Middle East and
Mayan, Aztec and Inca empires. In short Wittfogel's erudition
utilizes the Orient as one enormous historical and contemporary
cautionary tale for the West. What the Orient has always been so it
remains in a seamless tradition.

   Marco Polo and Wittfogel remind us that Orientalism is a compendium, one that ranges over all subject areas, is influenced by
politics and literary convention just as it works through both and
has influences on both spheres in its own turn. The history of
Orientalism is the history of the Western self, its ideas, doings, concerns and fashions, and it is present in all its forms whether overt or
covert. Conventionally Western history begins with a summation of
the legacy of knowledge it retained from ancient Greece and Rome.
So a history of Orientalism should commence with the limitations
of Greek and Roman knowledge of the Orient, ancient Orientalism. While it is true many features of Orientalism retain the icono-
clastic attitudes, ideas and knowledge of Greece and Rome, the
convention of beginning a history at that point is merely another

operation of Orientalism itself. The convention serves to demonstrate the Otherness of the Orient, its separation from the Western
birth and discrete identity of Western self-consciousness. The convention neatly obfuscates the actual origin of Orientalism in a crisis
of Western self-consciousness. The crisis demanded the creation of
a conception of the Orient that would permit its palpable threat to
the entire edifice of Western understanding to be distanced, denigrated and placed beyond, in the outer darkness where it belonged.
Whatever threads of Greece and Rome endure, and they do endure
even today, the history of Orientalism begins with the history of
Islam, with the crisis of the new, the unprecedented and inherently
subversive to which an urgent answer had to be found. Only in the
context of this crisis could Europe mobilize all it called its own,
including the legacy of Greece and Rome, to create a concept, a
form of surrogate self-definition, that is also the convention of
description and stance towards that which is not the Western self,
or the West, but is the Orient.

Islam and other monsters

From its inception, Islam presented the Christian world with a
'problem'. What was the purpose of the new revelation to an Arabian prophet over 600 years after the crucifixion and resurrection of
God's own son? Islam contained within itself a recognition of Christianity and its legitimacy: it described itself as the summation of the
messages brought by Abraham, Moses, Jesus and all the other
prophets; it accepted the virgin birth of Jesus and gave him a pres-
tigious position among the prophets; it accepted the Bible as one of
the books of God (although contaminated by human tampering).
Islam had no 'problem' with Christianity and from its inception
kept churches open and provided all the necessary guarantees for
the survival of Christianity and its institutions in Muslim lands. But
Christianity could not return this ecumenical courtesy. Europe was
still proselytizing the Christian faith within its own boundaries,
struggling to establish an orthodoxy that came to be based on the
exclusive claims of the Christian message and of the Church, as the
body of Christ, to be the vehicle of God's providence on earth.
When, within 100 years of Islam's inception, Europe found it at its
borders, Islam became a political problem. In addition, the achievements of Muslim civilization made Islam an intellectual, social and

cultural problem. Orientalism emerged as Europe's rationale for meeting the challenge of Islam.

The foundation of Orientalism was laid by John of Damascus (*d.*748), a Christian scholar who was a great friend of the Ummayad Caliph Yazid. He declared Islam to be a pagan cult, the Ka'aba in Makkah an idol, and the Prophet Muhammad an irreligious and licentious man. He claimed Muhammad cobbled together his doctrine from the Old and New Testaments through the instruction of an Arian monk. The writings and accusations of John of Damascus became the classical source of all Christian writings on Islam. Orientalism has proved to be a most retentive framework, few of its elements have entirely disappeared, so John of Damascus, the earliest exponent, could be said to be the guiding source and spirit of a recent study, *Hagarism* by Patricia Crone and Michael Cook,[5] that employs his structure of argument and assessment of the origin of Islam and, one should add, his animus. The pronouncement of John of Damascus found an echo in Christendom not only because it saw Islam as a distinctly different religion, but also because Muslim society reflected a totally different lifestyle to the one dominant in Europe. As R.W. Southern explained:

> For the greater part of the Middle Ages and most of its area, the West formed a society primarily agrarian, feudal, and monastic, at a time when the strength of Islam lay in its great cities, wealthy courts and long lines of communication. To Western ideals, essentially celibate, sacerdotal and hierarchical, Islam opposed the outlook of a laity frankly indulgent and sensual, in principle egalitarian, enjoying a remarkable freedom of speculation, with no priests and no monasteries built into the basic structure of society as they were in the West.[6]

Faced with a rapidly expanding new religion that produced a totally different form of society, which appeared to challenge God's promise to the Christian faithful, what could the leaders of Christendom do? They turned to the Bible. In the Book of Daniel, Paul Alvarus (*d.*859) discovered that Islam would flourish for only three-and-a-half periods of 70 years each; that is, 245 years in all. As he was writing in 854, and the Islamic calendar began in 622, it was not difficult for him to conclude that the end of the world was at hand. By a curious coincidence, in 852 the Emir of Cordova, Abd ar-Rahman III, died and was succeeded by Mahomet I, who was widely described in Christendom as 'the man of damnation of our time'.[7]

Alvarus and his colleagues possessed a brief biography of 'Mahomet', a parody of the life of Jesus, written by Spanish monks, which gave the year of Mahomet's death as 666 of the Spanish era. The year 666 is, of course, the number of the Beast of Revelations, the Antichrist. The picture was now complete. Thus was born the image of Muhammad as an Antichrist and of Islam as a sinister conspiracy against Christianity. This was, as Southern notes, 'the first and rigidly coherent and comprehensive view of Islam ... to be developed in the West'. It was a product of total ignorance, but an ignorance of a particular kind:

> The men who had developed this view were men writing of what they had deeply experienced, and they related their experience to the one firm foundation available to them – the Bible. They were ignorant of Islam, not because they were far removed from it like the Carolingian scholars, but for the contrary reason that they were in the middle of it. If they saw and understood little of what went around them, and they knew nothing of Islam as a religion, it was they who wished to know nothing.[8]

Wilful misunderstanding and knowledgeable ignorance have remained the guiding spirit of Orientalism, it has survived defiantly and remained dominant when alternative information has been readily available. Orientalism is composed of what the West wishes to know, not of what can be known. Once created the Orientalist image grew more and more entrenched as Islam continued to expand.

With the arrival of the Crusades, new imaginative flights of fancy were added to expand the propagandists' image of Islam as a tool to maintain the crusading spirit. Pope Urban preached the first Crusade at Clermont in France in 1096. He anchored the new idea of Crusading in some old and well-established European ideas: good works and pilgrimage. He also established the seminal building blocks of European self-consciousness by asserting the Christian right to dominance over the territory which was the birthplace of Christianity and once part of the Christian Roman Empire. His frame of reference was a monolithic Christendom opposed to a monolithic Islam, its enemy. The preaching of the Crusade provoked a genuine European response, it set a great cross-section of the population on the move for the Holy Land. As Gwyn A. Williams put it: 'A blend of zeal and greed of colonialism and an

aspiration for holiness, the Crusades dominated European imagination'.[9] So great a hold did the Crusades have on the popular
imagination that the crusading ethos became a central motif of
Western thought and literature that endured centuries after actual
campaigns into the Middle East had ceased. The physical place
sought by the Crusades was intimately familiar to all Europeans.
The Middle East is the land described in the Bible. Pilgrimage
literature as devotional text and guidebook was a major genre of
European letters, with a marked tendency to concentrate on
descriptions of places associated with miracles, long before the
Crusades gave a new twist to this tradition. In an imaginative and
figurative sense this land already belonged to Christian peoples, the
Crusades made a literalist leap by arguing for the right to actual
dominance.

The idea of the journey of life as pilgrimage to the heavenly New
Jerusalem seamlessly became the Crusading ideal of conquest and
dominance aimed at the centre of the Earth, the terrestrial
Jerusalem, into the east that became the Orient. The Crusades
would have been unimaginable, unthinkable except for the existence of Islam. As deeply as the Crusading motif entered into European consciousness so too did the opposing elements of Islam; they
were inextricably bound, the one had no rationale without the
other. Whether as triumphalism or valiant defiance of a small, iso-
lated, embattled enclave – and crusading ideas held both notions –
the palpable sense of an enemy was essential and entered as deeply
into the construction of the Crusading ideal. The black propaganda
consciously created to further the cause of the Crusades built on
pre-existing knowledgeable ignorance of Islam and radically
expanded it. The Crusaders brought with them not knowledge but
fairy-tales designed to focus hostility towards those who held sway
on the ground where Christ had walked. Now Mahomet was a
magician who destroyed the Church in Africa and the East. He
attracted converts to his depraved religion by promising them
promiscuity. He finally met his end, during one of his fits, with a
herd of pigs. At his death a white bull appeared to put the fear of
Christ in his followers and carry away Mahomet's laws in his horns.
Mahomet's tomb was suspended in mid-air by magnets.

The First Crusade achieved the sack of Jerusalem in 1099. This
led to the establishment of Crusader kingdoms in the Middle East
that remained in existence for over two centuries; Jerusalem itself

did not fall back into Muslim hands until 1244, Acre fell in 1291. The Crusades were not a simple there-and-back-again pilgrimage journey. It was a process of involvement extending over centuries, constantly replenished by new Crusades and new waves of personnel from Europe. The essential feature of this prolonged involvement is its ideological content that was continually refreshed and reiterated to sustain physical and financial support for Crusading and Crusaders as well as to prevent those resident in the Middle East from 'going native'. So Crusading bequeathed to Orientalism the distorted imagination, constructed misrepresentation that precluded closer contact becoming a vehicle for improved mutual understanding. Indeed, one might say contact itself became the 'problem' that required conceptual distance, the making of Islam 'into something it could not possibly be', as Norman Daniels has called it. One element of this constructed ignorance, as Daniels has shown, was the cycle of popular performance literature known as the *chansons de geste*, where the Prophet Muhammad was first given the Devil's synonym, Mahound. One of the oldest *chansons de geste* is *The Song of Roland*, written by Cretien de Troyes *circa* 1130. It espouses the Crusading ideal by invoking history, it sets the antipathy to Islam back to the era of the Battle of Rancevals in 778, in the world of Charlemagne, the fictive birth of the idea of Europe. It describes Muslims as pagans who worship a trinity of gods alongside Mohomme. The actual gods Tervagent, Apolin and Jupiter partake of features of Celtic gods, as Gwyn A. Williams argues, so that the development of Arthurian romances and Crusade literature mingles and merges inextricably. While the Crusades were a major movement against Islam, they were also a movement within Europe against enduring pockets of paganism and against heretics. Underlying *The Song of Roland* and the *chansons de geste* in general is the assumption that the world of the 'Saracens' is a mirror-image of Christendom, structured in exactly the same way but inverted in every moral sense. Thus, a valorous Saracen would have been an ideal *chevalier* had he been a Christian. When the hero Roland dies he offers his soul freely to archangels, but when the Saracen Marsilla dies his soul has to be wrestled from him by 'lively devils'.

The long period of interaction with Muslim civilization in Spain and the Crusader kingdoms made Europe a substantial borrowing society from its enemy. The East was rich in gold and jewels and new products that were avidly introduced into Europe to become necessities. But it was not merely a question of merchandise. The concept of the university was appropriated wholesale in form, terminology and course matter from the *madrassas* as they had developed from the eighth century onwards in the Muslim world. Muslim scholars had retained and built upon the learning of the classical world that had been lost to Europe. So avid was the desire for Arabic learning that underpinned the twelfth-century Renaissance, the age of Aquinas, Peter Abelard and Roger Bacon, that the authorities became seriously worried about the impact these unacceptable, heretical ideas were having on the fabric of learned Christendom. The propagandists had to take to their task again, with even greater vigour. In contradistinction to the passion for Arabic poetry stood the poetics of Dante Alligheri (1265–1321 CE). In canto 28 of *The Inferno* we encounter 'Maometto':

> No cask ever gapes by loss of end-board or stave like him I saw who was ripped from the chin to the part that breaks wind; between the legs hung the entrails; the vitals appeared, with the foul sack that makes excrement of what is swallowed. While I was all absorbed in the sight of him he looked at me with hands laid upon his breast saying: 'See now how I split myself; see how Mahomet is mangled!' Before he goes Ali in tears, his face cleft from chin to forelock; and all the others thou seest here were in life sowers of scandal and schism and therefore are thus cloven. . . .

The influence of Muslim philosophers was also being felt. The view of Islamic philosophy articulated strongly by Avicenna (ibn Sina), that man can never have a direct audience with God, began to gain a small foothold in academic quarters of Christendom. It brought forth an orthodox riposte from St Thomas Aquinas, in a lengthy discussion written about 1250. But to defend his theological position, that the souls of the blessed enjoy a direct vision of God, Aquinas had to depend on another Muslim philosopher, Averroes (ibn Rushd). If the error was inspired by Avicenna, the language and methodology of the retort was supplied by Averroes. For Aquinas, Muslims and Jews were invincibly ignorant, having heard the message of Christianity and rejected it, as opposed to the vincibly ignorant peoples, those who had not come into contact with the proselytizing message. Roger Bacon (*d.*1292) saw it as his task to use Islamic philosophy to launch a mission of preaching against Islam. 'Philosophy is a special province of the unbeliever: we have it all from them', he declared.[10] But his efforts fell on the ears of a deaf Pope. John Wycliffe, writing in 1378–84, saw Islam not just as theological heresy, but also a heresy at the level of morals and practice. Christianity had become the measure of 'normal' ways of life, life lived according to natural law. John of Segovia (*d*.1458) thought Islam should be tackled at the fundamental level of the Qur'an. The basic question was, is the Qur'an the word of God or not? If by examination of its text it could be shown to contain contradictions, confusions, errors, traces of composite authorship these should convince anyone that it was not what it claimed to be. The Council of Vienna in 1312 argued that Muslims could not be converted by persuasion or by the sword since their hearts were hardened, they despised the Scriptures, they rejected argument, they clung to the tissue of lies of the Qur'an. Therefore, it was proposed that an academic onslaught should be launched on the Saracens, that Arabic professorships should be established at Paris, Oxford, Bologna and Salamanca. The decree was repeated in Basle in 1343, but the chairs of Arabic did not come into existence until the middle of the seventeenth and early eighteenth centuries.

The crusading presence in the Middle East opened the way for travel writing to develop as a hybrid form of pilgrimage literature. Those who wrote of their travels were a diverse cross-section of European society: missionaries; men of rank on missions of state: merchants and traders, seeking profit from the undoubted riches of the East; as well as later-day pilgrims in the conventional sense and those making an intellectual pilgrimage – the Grand Tour, travel to broaden the mind, is a tradition born in the medieval period. One might say the guiding spirit of this travel writing is a compilation distilled from Guibert of Nogens and St Bernard. Guibert of Nogens wrote a biography of Muhammad, which he admitted was based on imagination, though he thought it safe to speak evil of someone who was clearly the Antichrist. St Bernard saw Christ glorified in the death of a Muslim. The land where miracles had happened, the Holy Land of the East, effortlessly became a land of wonders. The model was the popular eleventh-century *Wonders of the East*, a forerunner of the medieval bestiaries, that recorded all the varieties of monstrous races of humanity, a concept inherited from classical times, who lurked on the eastern fringes of European

experience. The East referred to in this work is Egypt and Baby-
lonia, the surrounding territory of the centre of the earth, the
middle, hence Middle East, that is the Holy Land. As Mary B.
Campbell notes, '"The East" is a concept separable from any
purely geographical area. It is essentially "Elsewhere".'[11] For
medieval and later Orientalist writers, as for their classical fore-
bears, the location of the monstrous races moved from place to
place, from Orient to Orient according to the accidents of contact
and interest. It was the existence of the monstrous races, cannibals,
troglodytes, dog-headed people and the like, that was essential and
enduring, a trope that symbolized conceptual distance, that placed
the Orient outside the West and made it meaningful for Western
purposes. Travel writing might be called a 'secular' genre but it
expressed the secular preoccupations of a particular society, it
emerged from the consciousness and imagination of its own contemporary society and deployed that society's values, aspirations
and perceptions. It tells us what medieval society thought it important to notice and know. In the medieval period all writing had
moral purpose, and the greatest moral purpose of all was the distinction of good and evil, the clear identification of devilish tricks
and imitations from heavenly signs. St Augustine himself had given
warrant to this outlook, acknowledging the monstrous races as an
object lesson, a heavenly sign of God's creative power. They were
conceptually rich symbols, engraved on maps, in the marginalia of
books to become a consistent part of the expectations of all who
travelled beyond the bounds of Europe. The traveller saw what he
expected to see, and reported what his audience at home had been
conditioned to expect, would be interested in and diverted by.
Everything had to be described through the straitjacket of medieval
scholastic technique, the ascription of similarity and difference, a
technique that underscored and reified Europe as the measure and
norm of all things. The Florentine Ricoldo da Montecroce went to
Baghdad in 1291 and was totally blind to Muslim learning and intellectual achievements, which at the time represented the zenith of
civilization. His major concern was to attack Islam, which he called
lax, and Muslims whom he described as confused, mendacious,
irrational, violent, obscure and so on. The Irish Franciscan, Simon
Semeonis, travelled to Palestine in 1323 with a copy of the Qur'an
which he often quoted; but he could not mention the name of
Mahomet once without such opprobrious epithets as pig, beast,

son of Beliel, sodomite and so on. And then there was Sir John Mandeville, the doyen and model of all travel writers, patron and archetype of all Orientalists.

Involvement with the Orient of Islam built up such a wealth of material on the East it was not even necessary for a 'traveller' to leave his own fireside. A major part of the Orientalist canon is provided by the speculations, imagination and writing in all genres of those who have never had any direct contact with the Orient except through books. Books speaking to books solidified the distorted imagination of knowledgeable ignorance into the concrete foundations of the Western self-consciousness and its informational repertoire. This is the position held by Sir John Mandeville who, according to his account, left St Albans on Michaelmas 1356. In fact, probably, there was no such person and whoever wrote the most famous and long-lived travel book of all time never went further east than his library. The longevity of Mandeville's *Travels* perplexes many modern scholars, who try to disavow its medieval flights of fancy and search for rationalist underpinnings that were built on by more scientific readers in later ages. It all misses the point magnificently. The last known reworking of *The Travels* was published in 1785, it has stout yeoman Sir John leaving St Albans in 1732! The entire text is presented as contemporary, as if four hundred years had not happened, because in the most important conceptual sense they were quite irrelevant. By 1785 the Enlightenment had happened, science had been born and the whole terrestrial globe had been visited, reported on and after a fashion had become known and/or conquered by Europe. As Percy Adams has made clear travel lies and travel liars were taken for fact, often in preference to what we would call 'reality' readily available from other sources. So Thomas Pennant in his encyclopaedic *Outlines of the Globe* (1798–1800) could describe Mandeville as 'the greatest traveller of his or any other age'. Reading travellers' tales began and remained, indeed remains, guided not by rationalism, scientism and veracity but the conceptual requirements of the Orientalist understanding crafted by the Orientalist imagination, exactly the point understood and exploited by whoever wrote *The Travels of Sir John Mandeville*.

The object of *The Travels* is pilgrimage to the Holy Land, so it is founded firmly in tradition. Pilgrimage texts as guidebooks were forms of encyclopaedia; true to the genre Sir John includes Biblical and classical learning about each place he mentions. These places are suspended in time, the sense of history as change had not yet been invented; there is also a great disinterest in the contemporary life going on in the Middle East, a common feature of much medieval writing. What matters first and foremost is the Biblical association of these places and their association with European history. Sir John therefore records the career of St Helena, mother of the Emperor Constantine, who invented many of the Biblical locations that became pilgrimage sites and cannot help informing us she was British, the beautiful daughter of King Coel. What is most interesting is that Sir John gives a significantly tempered humanist reading of Islam. He is able to acknowledge Muslim belief in the virgin birth and the respect given to the Virgin Mary and Jesus. He makes a fable from John of Damascus' explanation of the origin of Islam. He read carefully, picking and choosing his sources, distilling from the whole breadth of writing on Islam available. He is able to give a cogent presentation of what Muslims believe that leads him to the, perhaps ironic, conclusion that they are capable of conversion. He also presents an account of Muslim history, an annals of the Sultans, as a bloodthirsty tale of murder, poisonings and rapine. He then presents a private conversation he had with The Sultan – and thus generates a whole genre of Orientalist writing. The Sultan is made to bemoan the corrupted state of Christianity in Europe, a tale the writer cannot deny:

> It seemed to me then a cause of great shame that Saracens, who have neither a correct faith nor a perfect law, should in this way reprove us for our failings, keeping their false law better than we do that of Jesus Christ; and those who ought by our good example to be turned to the faith and Law of Jesus Christ are driven away by our wicked ways of living.[12]

The Sultan had obviously learned of the state of Europe from the spies he sent undercover as merchants to 'spot out our weaknesses'. Like so much else he wrote this aspect of Sir John would loom large down the ages of the Orientalist tradition, using the non-Christian non-European Orient to berate the contemporary state of life and society in the West. From the Middle East Sir John goes on to travel over all the known world: to India, China, Southeast Asia ending his journey at the ultimate east, the borders of the terrestrial Paradise.

Encyclopaedic in scope Sir John includes all of the monstrous races in his litany of places to the east of the middle, and much geographic knowledge. *The Travels* was first printed in 1470. It was avidly read by Christopher Columbus who found within it confirmation of the spherical world and the idea that one could sail to the East via the West. Dr Chanca, the ship's surgeon on Columbus's second voyage, in his account of the journey repeats almost word for word a section from Mandeville's *Travels*. The human battery farms where cannibals fatten their victims, which Mandeville located in Southeast Asia, are explained to Dr Chanca by an 'Indian' of the Caribbean, while the interpreter, who spoke Hebrew and Arabic, was absent and the two conversationalists had no mutual language, an apt example of the Orientalist process. Because of its Biblical association, for Europe the Orient was always first and foremost the Middle East. All other Easts were arrived at via this portal. When Columbus followed Mandeville's directions Europe was confronted by a new 'Present Terror of the World', as Francis Bacon called it: Ottoman expansion into Europe. Islam was the major force propelling European exploration of the globe. Driven out of the Holy Land and beset by new inroads that called for pan-European defence in Austria and the Balkans and economically dependent on the Muslim lands, Europe longed to break the stranglehold of its isolation. A compelling motive was to seek direct access to the gold it had to import from the Maghreb to pay for the produce of the East acquired in the Levant and thus change Europe's appallingly bad terms of trade with the Muslim world. Another was the search for Prester John, a supposed Christian monarch somewhere out East, or for the Great Cham of Marco Polo, another potential ally against the Ottomans. Columbus's fortuitous stumbling upon the Americas and the intellectual as well as spiritual ferment caused by the Reformation, which all happened within a generation, enabled Europe to change the dynamic of its relations with the East. Had it not been for the landfall in the Americas the project of attaining 'the Indies' would have been an entirely depressing undertaking. Not only was Prester John not found but the Portuguese coast-hugging voyages eastwards finally made landfall on the most Muslim part of the Malabar coast of India, at Calicut. Vasco da Gama's little flotilla was guided there from the Muslim ports of East Africa by a Muslim pilot. Trading privileges in India had to be arranged with the Muslim Mughal

Court. Melaka, the Malaysian city that Tomas Pires described as a cornucopia of riches, the greatest entrepot port in the world, was the seat of a Muslim sultanate. And in the Spice Islands themselves, the Moluccas, would-be traders found themselves playing off the rivalries of the Muslim sultans of Ternate and Tidor. In the face of this new Orient it was the spirit of Europe and European self-perception that changed to make the next era of Orientalism an era that in many respects has not yet ended.

The combined forces of Renaissance, Reconnaissance and Reformation produced a whole new stance towards the non-West. New lands and their peoples threw up perplexing questions about history and human origins, indeed the definition of human nature and natural life and laws. The Reformation, the most potent reformulation of all, required answering anew the entire framework of Western understanding from the purpose and meaning of existence to the nature and origins of the world. The intellectual resources for this project of enquiry, from which emerged the rationalist scientific worldview, were provided by the basic sources of Western thought: the Bible and the classical heritage of ancient Greece and Rome. All the Orients and Indies became the 'reserved laboratory' from which new information was gleaned to resolve the major questions of Western self-consciousness, from which new speculation was manufactured, tested and claimed to be proved. Reserved laboratory is Ernest Gellner's term for the attitude of anthropologists to their subject matter, but it is equally applicable, indeed the most apposite term for the outlook of Orientalists especially from the sixteenth to the eighteenth century when the modern concepts of the West were being formulated. Very quickly, and with meagre justification, Reformed and Counter-Reformed Europeans claimed to have progressed, not only beyond the achievements of the Ancients but also beyond the achievements of the great civilizations of the Orient: Islam, India and China. All of medieval Orientalism, its preoccupations, attitudes and techniques were retained, indeed were fundamental ingredients in effecting the transformation of Western self-perception and knowledge, while they enabled the Orient as a whole to be inexorably transmuted from rich, powerful and superior to markedly poor, viciously incompetent and inferior. The complete revision took centuries, centuries of preoccupation with Western internal problems, centuries during which modernity was constructed using the building blocks shaped and facilitated by dominance over and involvement with the non-West, the Orient.

The study of the Middle East, the medieval Orient, attained new significance. Arabic language was considered essential to improve knowledge of ancient Hebrew, an aid to translations of the Bible into European vernaculars instead of Vulgate Latin. The way of life and customs of the contemporary Orient were seen as an essential aid to interpreting the life of Biblical times in those lands. Sir John Chardin, the French Protestant who settled in England after many years wandering about the Middle East, declared it was his 'favourite design' to 'prepare notes on very many passages of the Holy Scriptures, whereof the explication depends on knowledge of the custom of the eastern countries'.[13] So Archbishop Laud, a fulcrum of the English Reformation, endowed an Arabic Chair at Oxford and made a major collection of Arabic manuscripts, which eventually passed to the Bodleian Library, as well as being an ardent supporter of Edward Pococke, first Professor of Arabic at Oxford. In Cambridge the first Chair of Arabic was established in 1632, its occupant was William Bedwell. His duties, established by the Head of Houses in Cambridge, were: (1) 'the advancement of good literature by bringing to light much knowledge which is lockt up in that learned tonge'; (2) 'good service of King and State in our commerce'; and (3) 'in God's good time to enlarging the borders of the Church, and propagation of the Christian religion to them who now sitt in darkness'.[14] Bedwell, who is regarded as the father of Arabic studies in Britain, had a good command of Arabic and a reasonable reservoir of sources on Islam and Muslims. But what are authentic documents worth in the face of intense hatred? As Alastair Hamilton, Bedwell's biographer, noted:

> The gratuitous venom which Bedwell expends on Islam at every opportunity, even in his dictionary, is striking in its intensity. A manifest exhibition of his attitude can be seen in the title Mohammedis Imposturae in the first edition, and Mahomet Unmasked in the second, with the recurrent subtitle, 'A Discovery of the manifold forgeries, falsehood and horrible impieties of the blasphemous seducer Mohammad: with a demonstration of the insufficiencies of his law, contained in the cursed Alkoran'.[15]

In the new reformed perspective of Europe religion became even more central to self-definition and understanding. Humphrey

Prideaux, Dean of Norwich, writing in 1697, saw Muslims as part of God's inscrutable purposes: to be a punishment for the sins of Christians.[16] Therefore, the great Islamic Empires of Turkey, Persia and Mughal India continued in existence: 'a scourge to us Christians who, having received so holy and so excellent a religion through His mercy to us in Jesus Christ our Lord, will not yet conform ourselves to live worthy of it'.[17] To Prideaux, Muhammad was 'an illiterate barbarian'.[18] The animus and attitudes would have been familiar to Pope Urban. Prideaux's contemporary, Peter Heylyn, considered the Qur'an 'a thing so full of tautologies, incoherencies, and such gross absurdities of so impure and carnal mixture, that he must lay aside the use of his natural reason who is taken in by it'.[19] As befits such a seminal writer as Heylyn his assessment links the consensus of the medieval period with that of the Enlightenment and nineteenth-century students of natural philosophy and echoes on down to today.

The Christian sense of superiority, the Reformed notion of being the 'elect of God', and opprobrium for Islam were constant features. But the sense of social and scientific advance was something new. One of the many threads that enabled this new fabric to be woven was the Ottoman Empire itself. In the medieval period Europe had been acutely aware of the superior learning of Muslim civilization, but no such obligation applied to the Ottomans, who were most often described as Tartars deriving from Scythia, known as the home of vicious barbarians since classical times. So Robert Huntingdon was able to sum up the new consensus in a letter written from Aleppo to John Locke: 'The country is miserably decay'd and hath lost the reputation of its name, and the mighty stock of credit it once had for eastern wisdom and learning: it hath followed the motion of the sun, and is universally gone westward.'[20] It was the constantly reiterated mantra, from Vico to Herder to Hegel. The ascendancy of Europe and the West was in every meaningful sense a battle won at the expense of the East, a continuation of the conceptual interrelations of east and west. The Turks were crude philistines: 'people generally of the grossest apprehension, knowing few other pleasures but such sensualities as are equally common both to man and beasts' according to Henry Maundrell.[21] 'They improve not sciences much, and it is enough for them to read and write', said Andre de Thevenot.[22] Arab astronomy had become Turkish astrology. 'For other sciences as logick, physick, metaphysick, mathematicks and other of our university learning, they are wholly ignorant' said Sir Paul Rycaut, English Consul in the Levant.[23] Turkish society was also the model on which Oriental despotism was constructed. Sir William Temple thought the Ottoman Empire 'the fiercest in the world'.[24] The Sultan was an absolute ruler sustained by ministers who were slaves rather than an hereditary aristocracy. They owed their appointment to his whim and might lose their lives at his slightest displeasure. The core of the army was the slave regiments. From the highest to the lowest obedience was enforced by cruelty and terror. No one enjoyed security. The end result was poverty and devastation, a population constantly pillaged by the government had no incentive to produce beyond its barest wants. Again that Orient which was closest to Europe and most feared by Europe acquired the character that eventually marked all other Orients.

Assessments of Ottoman rule created the lens through which all Orients could be viewed. So François Bernier, the uncontested expert on the Mughals who served as a physician at the Mughal Court, could link the Ottomans to Persia and Mughal India and conclude that 'Actuated by a blind and wicked ambition to be more absolute than is warranted by the laws of God and of nature, the kings of Asia grasp at everything, until at length they lose everything.'[25] So in India too a fertile country with a favourable balance of trade under Mughal government produced poverty and lands went uncultivated. The other aspect of Ottoman behaviour that found constant reiteration, along with their sensuality and effeminacy, was their harsh treatment of non-Muslims. There is a strong whiff of irony in these judgements on the Orient made in the so-called Age of Reason. The actual state of learning in Europe had advanced very little from the knowledge and ideas it had imbibed from Muslim civilization. Alchemy remained the major preoccupation of even such luminaries as Isaac Newton, who was also fascinated with Biblical chronology. And in complaining of the harsh treatment of Christians by the Ottomans surely Europe was ascribing its own worst failing to its enemy, given the horrors of the Reformation wars and the treatment of its new non-Christian subject peoples in the Americas. The history of Orientalism includes a specific form of disassociationism. The Orient is a discrete category, a utility for the internal speculations of and about the Western self and society, yet extraneous to that self and society,

separable from it. So Sir John Chardin, who took such interest in
the contemporary customs of the Orient for the supreme purpose
of proper understanding of the Scriptures, argued knowledge of the
customs of the people of India was 'in no ways useful itself'. What
was useful only for the purposes of the West could be favourably
esteemed, without making any dent in the overriding animus and
distaste for the peoples of the Orient themselves. The antiquity of
the East could be valued and admired for its utility in resolving the
central questions of Western existence while the present occupants
of the Orient as pagan barbarians were uniformly denigrated.
Orientalism was a device for picking and choosing. One cannot
select what appear to be favourable comments and attitudes and
take them as the footprints of a kind of 'Whig history', the birth
pangs of today's political correctness. The favourable is embedded
firmly in its total context. Those who thought well of the Orient
were always marginal and the seemingly admiring was balanced by
the what was taken to be coherently objectionable. So Thevenot
could comment 'In Christendom many think the Turks are devils,
barbarians and men of no faith and honesty, but such as know and
have consorted with them, have a different opinion . . . They are
devout and charitable; very zealous for their religion.'[24] Fanatical
attachment to false religion was considered the major failure of the
Orient, a major ingredient of the stereotype. Individual rarities
were just that, individual, or more commonly making example of
the enemy to point out their fondest hope for reform of their own
society and its attitudes. Take Sir Thomas Baines's conversation
with Van Effendi, the Turkish teacher, Sir Thomas expressed the
opinion that:

> He believed a Musselman, living up to the height of his law, may be
> undoubtedly saved. He thought himself obliged . . . not to touch a hair
> of a Musselman's head for his difference of religion, but rather to help,
> assist, relieve and cherish them in every good office that he was able to
> do them. At which Van Effendi wept and said he could not believe any
> Christian came so near true Musselman but that they had all been idol-
> aters.[27]

The age of unreason

The Ottomans drew a line which separated unfortunate aspects of
the Middle East's past from its present and redoubled the sense of

antipathy. They created a platform from which to assess other Orients that had now become accessible to Europe, a comparative framework in which to look at India and China. The looking was as much preoccupied with the question of time, the reformulation of the history of the world as it was with the present utility of the newly available Orients for European ends both commercial and strategic. The new Orients were means to outmanoeuvre the Ottomans and arenas in which European mercantilist rivalries were played out. The Orient of Islam and the Ottomans determined attitudes to what was found in India and China. The Mughals were merely another variant of the Ottomans. The Hindu population of India attracted less attention. Edward Terry considered them 'very silly, and sottish, and an ignorant sort of people who are so inconsistent in their principles, as they scarce know the particulars they hold'.[28] They were undoubtedly an ancient people and therefore the consensus was that Hindus were the Gentiles spoken of in the Old Testament of the Bible, the Hindu pantheon supplying the meaning of idolatry spoken of there, hence the most common name for them, used for centuries, was Gentoo.

China was principally known through the accounts of the Jesuits and was marked by their particular concerns. There was no doubting Marco Polo's conclusion that China was a colossus, rich and populous. It was also not Muslim, a matter of some delicacy and a great opportunity if only the right means of conversion could be found. Initial Portuguese reports were coloured by the harrowing experiences of early missions to China, such as those of Galeote Pereira. His account of how his crew was arrested, many of its members executed and the great cruelties and tortures visited on those who were imprisoned and exiled to parts of South China reached the Jesuits in Goa. Included in their annual report, it was subsequently printed and translated across Europe. It established the cold-hearted cruelty of China firmly in the Western imagination. Pereira also reiterated one of Marco Polo's findings that became a standard feature of accounts of China: that sodomy was a vice 'very common in the meaner sort, and nothing strange amongst the best'.[29] The major influence on European information about China was the Jesuit Matteo Ricci, who opened the first mission there in 1583. The edited translation of his journals was published in 1616. Ricci's objective was conversion, so he had to attempt to understand Chinese civilization. He presented a portrait of a Confucian Empire that was well-ordered, organized and essentially benign. In contrast to the capriciousness of Muslim rulers the Chinese Emperor put the welfare of his people first, was open to advice and criticism and his rule attained an astonishing uniformity across the vastness of China through regular hierarchies of mandarins selected for their learning by public examination. China was governed like one large family. Of Confucius himself, Ricci wrote: 'if we critically examine his actions and sayings as they are recorded in history we shall be forced to admit that he was the equal of the pagan philosophers and superior to most of them'.[30] Confucianism was a moral framework, not a religion as such. A major obstacle to conversion was Buddhism, which Ricci discussed as a mass of primitive superstitions fostered by uneducated and often immoral priests; another was the deeply entrenched belief in astrology, which had replaced scientific astronomy; and the greatest impediment of all was ancestor worship. The Jesuitical answer was what became known as Chinese rites, a syncretic form of Catholicism. It was an adaptation of the Malabar Rites formulated in Goa, the seat of the Portuguese in India, that gave a measure of toleration to child marriage, Hindu insignia and names and caste segregation. In China, ancestor worship was redefined as acts of homage to the departed rather than religious invocation designed to obtain favours or benefits. The same was also deemed true of Chinese ritual ceremonies in the name of Confucius. Therefore the Chinese could retain such ceremonies, though they would have to give up their concubines before conversion could take place. Ricci also repeated the view of earlier accounts that homosexuality was common. Reporting on all the crafts and trades of China he observed that they had fallen behind the West in science because they 'have no conception of the rules of logic' consequently 'the science of ethics with them is a series of confused maxims and deductions'.

The Jesuit view of China held sway for a considerable time, though it was never uncontested and always controversial. The Dominican friar, Domingo Navarette, fell foul of the Jesuits in China and returned to Europe to vent his anger in a massive two-volume treatise appropriately called *Tratados e Contoversias*. He dubbed the new Manchu rulers of China Tartars, the conventional epithet for barbarians, creating another demarcation between past and present. For him, Chinese ingenuity along with their apprehension of science and learning was now little more than imitation, including imitation of European goods copied on the coast and sold in the interior as European produce. Despite the contrary evidence, the benign Jesuit image predominated. Its most powerful effect was on Gottfried Wilhelm Liebniz. Born in 1646 and growing up in the Germany of the cataclysmic Thirty Years War his interest in religion and logic was dedicated to seeking the balance of extremes, for which he found great compatibility in Chinese thought. He had been attracted to Chinese ideas by the hexagrams of the *I Ching*, which fitted very well with his binary arithmetic. While convinced of the claims of European science – 'in those matters we are superior' – he could eulogize Chinese 'precepts of civil society': 'indeed it is difficult to describe how beautifully all the laws of the Chinese, in contrast to those of other peoples, are directed to the achievement of public tranquillity and the establishment of social order so that men shall be disrupted in their relations as little as possible'.[31] Chinese 'practical philosophy' might redeem his own society because the Chinese moral sense expressed in Confucian and other values constituted a kind of 'natural religion'.

The Age of Reason was much concerned with forging the Western perception of scientific advance, the outcome of the battle of the Moderns and the Ancients. A concept of Western progress was the innate assumption of the Enlightenment, and it found its greatest prop in the equally firm assumption of the unchanging nature of the Orient. A new sense of history was developing in the West, a history that required the stasis of the Orient to provide its explanatory power. The battle over religious meaning was far harder to resolve for the West and it resulted in the application of some very old techniques, first pioneered in the explanation and investigation of Islam in the medieval period, to Christianity itself. Radical thinkers of the Enlightenment were indeed the very model for modernity in the West, and they were dedicated workers in the 'reserved laboratory' of the Orient. In defence of deism, natural religion and ridicule of the orthodox Christian history of the world they employed and deployed the Orient. They found in China, and to a lesser extent Hinduism, the lineaments of natural religion, and, what is more, a natural religion that seemed to predate the Bible and thus overturn the most central of all Christian claims, that of being the unique vehicle for God's providence. When Voltaire argued that behind the bizarre religions of India and China stood a concept of one God, the separation of body and soul and the immortality of the soul along

with a set of moral teachings, he established the contemporary definition of religion without any reference to the Bible, or Christianity.
Therefore, he created a platform for coherent opposition to the
obfuscation of clerics, a vehicle for major change not only in religious
thought but the social and political practice of Europe. Where the
Qu'ran had been investigated to discredit its claims by showing mul-
tiple authorship, internal contradictions, errors and confusions now
it was the Bible's turn.

The great matter, what created the 'problem' with orthodox
Christian ideas, was the claims for the antiquity of China and India.
The wealth of material that became available in the eighteenth
century included Indian assertions that put the origins of their
civilization back 4866 years. The content of Sanskrit texts was
made available to Europe through translation of the Persian translations of these texts. Knowledge of Sanskrit itself grew more hap-
hazardly and slowly and even among the supposed adepts could
lead to major errors. Nathaniel Brassey Halhed claimed, for
example, that Hinduism had no concept of the Flood, a feature of
all religions of the Middle East, ancient and more modern. In fact
it is included in the *Puranas*. The Hindu concept of time, divided
into four eras or *yugas*, gave the Earth an age of some eight million
years, a considerable advance on Archbishop Ussher's dating of
creation to 4086BC. Du Halde, most restrained and authoritative
of the Jesuits, gave the Chinese 4000 years of settled government
and sufficient scientific sophistication to record an eclipse of the
sun in 2155BC. This challenged the ruling orthodoxy, confirmed by
Isaac Newton, that the Jews were the oldest people on earth.
Defenders of orthodoxy found Chinese and Hindu religion easy
enough to fit within the dominant explanation. All the people of
the earth had a single origin in the Middle East, the Dispersion of
peoples had happened after the fall of the Tower of Babel, and any
similarities found between myths or religious ideas anywhere
could be explained by retention of ideas first learned before the
Dispersion. The problem, of course, is that the Dispersion comes
after the Flood and the date of the Flood, *circa* 2550BC, and Moses'
writing of the *Penteteuch*, *circa* 1600BC, were now claimed to come
after the origins of India and China, which were not mentioned in
the Bible. Sir William Jones, who founded the Bengal Asiatic
Society, settled the matter of chronology by comfortably resolving
the dating of India and China to make it conform to the orthodox

sequence. He also discovered great similarities between the structure of Sanskrit and Greek and Latin, and thus generated the
concept of Indo-European languages, a shared common origin far
in the past reflected not only in language but also mythology. Since
he traced the origins of the single language family to somewhere
in the Middle East he felt content he had confirmed the general
outlines of Genesis.

In the hands of the *philosophes*, and all who shared their intellectual temper, the Orient was a treasury of ideas for rethinking and
remodelling European attitudes and understanding. The eighteenth century was the high watermark of using the Orient to
reprove Europe, a coded means of satirizing and pointing out its
failures. While Daniel Defoe, whose *Robinson Crusoe* was taken
by many as fact not fiction, roundly abuses China others found it
conducive to accept the more flattering portrayals and use that as
a stick to beat their favourite whipping boys and advance their
favoured ideas. Oliver Goldsmith made his reputation with *The
Citizen of the World*, an epistolary novel told through a series of
letters between a Chinese scholar and his son. Addison, Steele,
Johnson and Horace Walpole all used Oriental settings for their
polemic writings. In England political debate was carried on
through satires set in harems and among the eunuchs of the court,
and so dense were the references to contemporary British political
figures that detailed explanatory keys were also published. The
satires made their point because corruption and venality were seen
as the natural concomitants of an Oriental court. Montesquieu used
the same premise when he produced his *Persian Letters*. Voltaire
satirized Liebniz, the model for his ever-optimistic Dr Pangloss, in
Candide. But Voltaire was just as ardent about China, producing in
1755 his play *Orphelin de la Chine*. It was the reworking of a translation of the Chinese story, *The Orphan of Chao*, but Voltaire
thought his resetting much superior to the original. He made the
play into a vehicle to demonstrate how the Mongol Genghis Khan
is eventually civilized by the order and values of Confucian China:
'I was a conqueror, now I am a king.' After his initial enthusiasm
for China, Voltaire discovered Hinduism in the 1760s thanks to a
manuscript called the 'Ezour Vedam', now known to be a forgery
'with beautiful appropriateness' produced by his great antagonists
the Jesuits. So he swiftly declared the Hindus the oldest people on
earth who had taught monotheism to the Chinese and invented the

concept of the separation of soul and body and the immortality of
the soul. Whatever utility the Orient possessed for resolving European problems there was an overriding consensus built and set into
concrete by the intellectual temper of the Enlightenment, the stasis
of the Orient in contrast to the progress of the West. In a sense it
is merely the rationalizing of the medieval European sense of perpetual contemporaneity, the lack of a perception of time as change.
This allowed early post-Columbian travellers to recycle the anec-
dotes of the classical heritage as well as medieval writings about far-
flung places as if nothing had or could have altered. The convention
was placed in the Orient, extended to all Orients and thus separated
from the Western self and its unique experience. Changing the
terms of existence was the intimate business of Western self-
consciousness, received ideas and the specific place assigned to the
Orient within the Western self-conception precluded any need to
extend the capacity for change to the object called the Orient.

Answering the question of the origin and history of the world
made the thinkers of the French and Scottish Enlightenment great
system builders. It was a convention of their thought that all ideas
and phenomena could be reduced to a single key that made them
work. The key to history was in a sense provided by its typology,
which came to be seen as a series of stages, and the stages grad-
ually became a developmental ladder. After all, the light in the
Enlightenment was that old flame being carried ever westward
from the ancient home of learning in the Orient, whichever Orient
an individual thinker happened to favour as first. As the light went
out in the East it left behind stagnation or, increasingly in later
eighteenth-century judgements, degeneration. The seminal work
was Montesquieu's *Spirit of the Laws* published in 1748. He saw
human history as reducible to three forms of government: mon-
archies, despotisms and republics; each directed by single principle:
honour, fear, virtue. So monarchy on the principle of honour produced hierarchy; despotism, on the principle of fear produced a
lone ruler who was a slave to his passions; republics, however, on
the principle of small-scale virtues lead to the growth of equality
among citizens. As much as this was a typology it was also an argument for the correct political development of Europe. It provided
the language and concepts from which nineteenth-century social
thought and social science would emerge: the threefold distinction
of mores, manners and laws. The typology came with explanatory

ideas such as the effect of climate on temperament, family structure, commerce, religion and history – the environmental thesis of
nineteenth-century social science. It all led to one overriding senti-
ment: in Asia strong and weak nations existed side by side therefore one must be conqueror the other conquered, quite unlike
Europe where consistent levels of courage marked all nations. This
increased the tendency 'for the liberty of Europe and servitude of
Asia; a cause that I think has never before been observed. This is
why liberty never increases in Asia, whereas in Europe it increases
or decreases according to their circumstances.'[32]

Voltaire echoed the judgement in his *History of Manners and
Spirit of Nations*, published in 1756, where he noted that China had
stagnated, 'we on the other hand, were tardy in our discoveries, but
then we have speedily brought everything to perfection'.[33] Adam
Ferguson in his 1767 *Essay on the History of Civil Society* (1986)
also followed the threefold division of history, his being savagery,
barbarism and civilization with Asia being firmly fixed in the
despotic mould that had expanded from the Ottomans to be the
consensus on all of Asia.[34] The eighteenth century opened with a
passion for chinoiserie, in Chinese gardens and decorations, tea
drinking and much more. 'If 18th century Englishmen envisaged
China as a willow pattern world of quaint figures crossing little
bridges, they were envisaging what was essentially a construct of
Europe's own imagination.'[35] The willow pattern was a design
taken to China for copying on porcelain destined for re-export to
Europe. But work in the 'reserved laboratory' made a marked
change by the end of the century. 'Ancient China stands as an old
ruin on the verge of the world', 'an embalmed mummy; wrapped
in silk and painted with heiroglyphs' governed by 'unalterably
childish institutions', according to Johann Gottfried von Herder.[36]
Marshall and Williams make the essential point:

> To assume that interpretations only changed as a result of new know-
> ledge would no doubt be unduly naïve. In fact, in the case of China,
> almost the reverse seems to be true. As far as Britain is concerned new
> knowledge was relatively limited during the 18th century but inter-
> pretation changed radically . . . It would be an exaggeration but one
> close to reality to argue that Europe 'made' and remade Asia in the
> 18th century to fit its own changing preoccupations rather than to sug-
> gest that European preconceptions were fundamentally altered by
> new knowledge of Asia.[37]

India too was to undergo revisionism. While travellers had never thought that well of the Hindu masses, Holwell found from practical experience that modern Hindus were as 'degenerate, crafty, superstitious, litigious, and wicked a people as any race of people in the known world'.[38] Yet he found the teaching of the shastah on the origins of moral evil to be 'rational and sublime' and the few Brahmins who actually lived the code were 'the purest models of genuine piety that now exist or can be found on the face of the earth', a distinction echoed by Abbé Reynal 'amidst a variety of absurd superstition, puerile and extravagant customs, strange ceremonies and prejudices we may also discover the traces of sublime morality, deep philosophy and refined policy'.[39] The early English students of 'philosophic' Hinduism, rigorously separated from 'popular' Hinduism that was not worthy of study, were all Christians of a marked Unitarian or dissenting stripe. They interpreted Hinduism as a kind of undogmatic Protestantism. Charles Wilkins, translator of the *Bhagavad Gita*, thought the Brahmins were Unitarians. As Marshall notes: 'All of them worked with contemporary European controversies very much in mind. As Europeans have always tended to do they created Hinduism in their own image. Later generations of Europeans interested themselves in mysticism were able to portray the Hindus as mystics'.[40]

But a century of intellectual endeavour created a new sense of confidence about the nature of Indian society; so without any acquaintance with its reality policy could properly be made for India in the British Parliament. Thus in 1781 Edmund Burke could take the lead on a parliamentary select committee in urging Parliament to restore peace to Bengal by giving Indians 'laws in accordance with the temper and manners of the people' and with the aid of Sir William Jones, who had not yet set foot in India, he felt able to draft a bill to protect Indians 'in the enjoyment of all those ancient laws and useages, rights and privileges'.[41] In fact, when it came to land reform the ancient laws and usages owed more to English usages in Burke's native Ireland than anything known in India. A continuous loop had been forged, one in which the reality of the Orient was entirely irrelevant because what was important to know was already available on the shelves of European libraries. Thus, men who ruled India down through the nineteenth century:

were men with strongly held prior beliefs expressed freely in the voluminous minutes and dispatches that they were required to send home
in which policy is frequently justified by sweeping assertions about
Indian society. Such assertions were rooted in the great body of writing about India from scholars and travellers alike which had been
accumulated through the 18th century as much as in actual obser-
vation of Indian conditions.[42]

What Marshall and Williams call the two greatest stereotypes of
Asia, the entire Orient – 'a continent of bizarre religions, fanati-
cally adhered to and it was a continent whose people changed very
little'[43] – were essentially judgements founded on the perceptions
of Muslim civilization that inexorably expanded to embrace all the
civilizations of Asia. The one stereotype explained the other as it
was their religions that required Orientals to remain forever the
same. The stasis of Asia was nothing more than the opinion of Sir
John Mandeville given four centuries earlier:

> And in this way this lord leads his life following the ancient custom of
> his ancestors which custom his successors follow in the same way. And
> thus they make their belly their god, so that they achieve no worthi-
> ness or bravery living only in pleasure and delight of the flesh, like a
> pig in a sty.[44]

Supposed knowledge had expanded the content of information
but not the judgement. When the rationalist temper of the Enlightenment succumbed to the blood-soaked horrors of the French
Revolution, Western disillusion with its own self produced the reac-
tion of romanticism, with its renewed emphasis on nostalgia for the
rustic antique; a nostalgia that increased as industrialism changed the
face of Europe. It provided a new rationale for interest in the
unchanging Orient. Contemporaneous with the Romantic Movement was the great upsurge of religious revivalism, the great evangelical awakening. The nineteenth century was *par excellence* a new
kind of missionary century. The revision of India and China, their
inclusion within the familiar lineaments of the static, decayed and
despotic constructed as the Islamic Orient made all Orients a fruitful field for missionary endeavour. The emphasis on decay became
the justification for the charitable impulse of the high Victorian era.
The militant conversion of the first Columbian era of Western expansion was inspired by seeking to add converts to the battalions opposing Europe's Islamic enemy. Increasing contact and involvement

with the Orient and the changed terms of Western self-perception gave a new twist to the missionary drive: offering the developmental balm of the progressive spirit that was the special possession of the West to the tyrannized peoples of the Orient. Missionary letters, magazines and tracts, produced to raise financial support for good works overseas, were the most common form of communication through which knowledge of the Orient came to the mass of the population in the West during the nineteenth century. Where in the eighteenth century the East India Company had resisted sending missionaries to India, a new breed of Company men, themselves infused with evangelical fervour, produced reports of India that led to a change in policy. The opinion of Charles Grant, a leading example, sums up the whole basis for the policy; he wrote: 'In fact, the people are universally and wholly corrupt, they are as depraved as they are blind, and as wretched as they are depraved.'[45]

The Orient on the canvas

Muslim civilization bequeathed another lens through which the popular image of the Orient was constructed. In 1704 Antoine Gallard published a translation called *Persian and Turkish Tales or 1001 Nights*, an English translation appeared in 1714. *Alf Laila wa Laila*, or the *Arabian Nights* as it is most commonly known, fed the imaginative sense of Europe. It personified the exotic Orient so well because it chimed in perfectly with all the travellers' tales and scholarly opinions already extant about the Orient, indeed that had been extant from the outset. It generated a fashion for such Oriental tales and many imitations quickly followed. By the early nineteenth century this imaginative Orient had become the conventional setting for pantomime: *Ali Baba, Sinbad, Aladdin and His Wonderful Lamp*, first performed on the stage in 1788, or Charles Dibdin's *Whang Fong* or *The Chinese Clown*. The West appropriated the Orient for its imaginative use for more than pantomime. The scholar's sense of dominance in knowledge about and interpretation of the Orient gave assurance to the appropriation of the travel writer, novelist, playwright and poet. They could begin to write through what they took to be the conventions, settings and language of the Orient. Writers such as Beckford, Southey and Moore read avidly all the scholarly works of Orientalists such as Sir William Jones, who produced numerous translations of Arabic and Persian poetry. When the Western literary self played at being an Oriental the fictive work confirmed and entrenched as well as it represented and deployed the received consensus on the nature and being of the Orient. It was the *Arabian Nights* projected back along with all the ideas about sensuality, licentiousness, cruelty, fanaticism, treachery, despotism and barbarism. The imaginative re-projection popularized and added force to the learned scholarly body from which it drew its sources and justification, another enclosed continuous feedback loop in which the reality of the Orient, any Orient, was quite irrelevant. Often European writers projected their own repressed sexuality onto their image of the Orient. For example, William Beckford's Oriental tale, *Vathek*, had a sinister, over-indulgent, wealthy young Caliph as its hero who allowed nothing to stand between him and his sexual appetites. But the story of the young Caliph is the story of Beckford himself, complete with Beckford's adulterous relationship with Louisa, wife of his cousin, portrayed by the relationship between Vathek and Nouronihar.

Received ideas about Islam and its Prophet now acquired the Oriental setting of the *Arabian Nights*. All the traditional hostility to Islam, including the description of Prophet Muhammad as an imposter and magician, can be seen, for example, in Thomas Moore's novel, *Lalla Rookh*, published in 1813. Moore made no attempt to differentiate between legend and history, having a Persian fire-worshipper denounce Muhammad as:

> A wretch who shrines his lust in heav'n
> And makes a pander of his God.[46]

No one has done more to harden the image of *Arabian Nights* as the reality of the Orient than Richard Burton. Like so many European travellers and adventurers, he sought gratification of his repressed sexuality in the Muslim world and maintained close links with the British government for espionage purposes. He projected every imaginable kind of sexual perversion onto the Orient. Burton presented Eastern women as sexual objects who were capable of infinite varieties of copulation and deserved equally infinite contempt:

> A peculiarity highly prized by Egyptians; the use of the constrictor vagina muscles, the sphincter for which Abyssinian women are famous. The 'Kabbazah' (holder), as she is called, can sit astraddle upon a man and can provoke the venereal orgasm, not by wriggling

and moving but by tightening and loosing the male member with the
muscles of her privities, milking it as it were.[47]

Thus, what you could not get in the Victorian home, Burton
announced to his contemporaries, you can find in the illicit space
that is the Orient. Burton had a great reputation, he had partici-
pated in the search for the source of the Nile, made a visit to Mecca
and Medina and been a distinguished servant of the East India
Company. The success of his translation of the *Arabian Nights*
taught him what really interested the reading public. So late in his
career he earned his richest financial rewards with translations, and
more footnotes, of the *Kama Sutra* and *The Perfumed Garden*.

Meanwhile, travel writing continued to reinforce the image of
Islam originally conceived by Paul Alvarus, added to by *chansons
de geste* and Humphrey Prideaux, sharpened by centuries of Orientalism, and served in the mould of Scheherazade. Thus, for de
Chateaubriand, fanaticism, barbarism, cruelty, despotism, servility,
violence, and unbelief came together in Muslim nations which
'belong essentially to the sword', and have a history that negates
civilization itself. Writes Hichem Djait:

> It would be hard to imagine a more Manichaean attitude than
> Chateaubriand's in the Itinerary from Paris to Jerusalem; he evoked
> all the passions of the mediaeval period, reaffirming it as he gloried in
> the splendours of a brutal and exclusive 'we', echoing, continuing, and
> reappropriating the Middle Ages as the core of a great tradition and a
> moment of truth in history.[48]

E.W. Lane described *Modern Egypt* as a treasure house of magic
and occult, astrology and alchemy, hemp and opium, snake-charm-
ers, jugglers, public dancers, superstitions, supernatural beliefs and
bizarre incidents that defied imagination. Beyond fanaticism, sex
and the bizarre there was always the old favourite: straight-to-the-
point contempt wrapped in a sense of moral and religious bigotry.
Doughty had total contempt for Islam and the people he mingled
with in *Travels in Arabia Deserta*. After declaring that the 'Moslem
religion ever makes numbness and death in some part of the human
understanding',[49] he ranted about the Prophet of Islam:

> The most venerable image in their minds is the personage of Moham-
> mad . . . [nothing can] amend our opinion of the Arabian man's bar-
> baric ignorance, his sleight and murderous cruelty in the institution
> of his religious faction; or sweeten our contempt of an hysterical

prophetism and polygamous living – Mohammad who persuaded others, lived confident in himself; and died persuaded by the good success of his own doctrine.[50]

In his introduction to the meanderings of Doughty, T.E. Lawrence wrote that Doughty 'went among these people dispassionately', 'the realism of the book is complete' as 'Doughty tried to tell the full and exact truth of all that he saw'. Lawrence highlighted Doughty's attitude to the Arabs by putting them in more precise terms:

Semites are black and white and not only in vision, with their inner furnishing; black and white not merely in clarity, but in apposition. Their thoughts live easiest among extremes. They inhabit superlatives by choice . . . They are limited narrow-minded people whose inert intellects lie incuriously fallow . . . They show no longing for great industry, no organisation of mind or body anywhere. They invent no system of philosophy or mythologies. . . . [51]

Prejudices, racism and bigotry found in literature and travel writing received empirical support from the colonial administrators. Cromer, for example, repeatedly insisted that 'the Egyptian Oriental is one of the most stupid . . . in the World . . . Stupidity, not cunning is his chief characteristic',[52] that the Egyptian mind 'like that of all oriental races, is naturally inaccurate and incapable of precision of thought and expression',[53] that the Oriental could only show a servile submission to authority, and, most of all, he was quite incapable of ruling himself. He devoted five chapters to delineating such features of the Oriental character in *Modern Egypt*:

Sir Alfred Lyall once said to me: 'Accuracy is abhorrent to the Oriental mind. Every Anglo-Indian should always remember that maxim.' Want of accuracy, which easily degenerates into untruthfulness, is in fact the main characteristic of the Oriental mind . . . The mind of the Oriental . . . is eminently wanting in symmetry. His reasoning is of the most slipshod description. Although the ancient Arabs acquired in a somewhat higher degree the science of dialectics, their descendants are singularly deficient in the logical faculty. They are often incapable of drawing the most obvious conclusions from any simple premises of which they may admit the truth.[54]

The *Arabian Nights* as well as the Turkish epics of Byron, Thomas Moore's Indian romance *Lalla Rookh*, Flaubert's *Salammbô*, Theophile Gautier's *La Roman de la Momie* and Victor Hugo's *Les*

Orientales and the travel accounts of Chateaubriand, Burton and
Alexandre Dumas *pere* – all of these provided a fertile soil for the
growth of the Orientalist school of painting. Byron wrote the *Turkish Tales* in 1811, after his return from the East. They are poems of
the gratuitous violence, irrational vengeance, and cold-hearted barbarity of Turks – representing the darker side of Romanticism. But
the Ottomans that Byron actually met were a different breed. As he
told the House of Lords:

> If it be difficult to pronounce what they [the Ottomans] are, we can at
> least say what they are not; they are not treacherous, they are not cow-
> ardly, they do not burn heretics, they are not assassins, nor has an
> enemy advanced to their capital. They are faithful to their sultan till he
> becomes unfit to govern, and devout to their God without an inquisi-
> tion. Were they driven from St Safia tomorrow, and the French or Rus-
> sians enthroned in their stead, it would become a question whether
> Europe would gain by the exchange. England would certainly be the
> loser.[55]

But his opinion did not inhibit Byron from supporting the independence movement of the Greeks which made him the great romantic icon.

Byron's literary Orient was one derived from the history of
Orientalism, a fictional image, a place of exotic fantasy, the kind of
fantasy that Byron created about his own persona. The fantasy
nourished a legion of Orientalist painters. The noted French
painter, Eugène Delacroix, for example, was inspired by Byron in
1827 to paint *La Mort de Sardanapale*. Based on a popular poem of
that name by Byron, the painting depicts an Oriental despot leaning
back on his lavish bed watching, rather apathetically, the destruction of his earthly possessions. All around him, his naked concubines are being stabbed and killed by three dark villains while his
horse is being dragged away. The chaos and violence of the narrative is coupled with eroticism: the concubines are dying in a state
of sexual ecstasy, their death is represented as an exotic spectacle,
observed voyeuristically both by Sardanapalus and us. Lane's
Modern Egypt became a source for many paintings of harem in-
teriors. The harem is one of the most powerful symbols of exoticism and Otherness associated with the Orient. It represents the
antithesis of all that the West believes about sexuality. The idea
finds its most coherent expression in the work of the classicist Jean

Auguste Dominique Ingres. As early as 1814, he had painted *Great Odalisque*, followed by his famous work *Odalisque and Slave* (1839) and *Turkish Bath* (1862). The *Great Odalisque* looks knowingly at the viewer: she knows she is the object of consumption and the subject of a gaze. She is passive, ready to receive, the mind and the body are simultaneously ready to be occupied. The paraphernalia of the harem is limited to an opium pipe and a hand fan of peacock feathers, while the cool blues and greens enhance the relaxed and luxurious atmosphere of the invitation – so evident in her eyes. The *Odalisque and Slave* takes the idea of total sensual gratification a step further. The woman in this painting has reached a sublime high, thanks to the opium from the water pipe beside her, the music played by the slave, the softness of the silk on which she lies, scent of perfume from the garden in the background, the tranquillity of the trees and the swan on the water, and the exquisite colours that surround her. Like Sardanapalus, she is oblivious to her fate. Come and conquer us! The *Turkish Bath* shows twenty-six nude women, in various stages of ecstasy, in a fantastic Turkish bath. The painting is round, depicting a double voyeurism of looking through a keyhole and picking up the roundness of the women's breasts and bellies. The gaze is unidirectional: the observer is looking at a private space but none of the women look out or look at each other.

> This voyeurism is an intrinsic part of the painting, for the onlooker has been presented with a means of gazing into a forbidden East. He enters a world of sexual abandon; he sees without being seen. The women in the painting all appear to be cloned from one model, as if depictions of one woman in an endless variety of poses. They are intertwined in love-postures, hinting at lesbian relationships. No bathing activity is actually visible; the bath here seems to be an occasion for undressing and dallying. The painting is an obvious collage of the hackneyed themes of Eastern sensuality; the women fondling each other, the perfumes, the incense, the music – all convey the endless potential of erotic gratification of such a lieu. The eroticism becomes, unintentionally no doubt, a parody of itself. For the compilation of bodies in a mass disturbs without arousing. It is a surplus which satiates.[56]

The female inhabitants of the harems and baths have a counterpart. Contrasting with the passive, inviting females, are the unrestrained and savagely barbaric males. The painting that perhaps most symbolizes the violent Muslim male is Henri Regnault's *A Summary Execution Under the Moorish Kings of Granada* (1870). When Regnault visited Granada in 1869, he was overwhelmed by the sheer beauty of the Al-Hambra. But his main interest was to 'depict the real Moors in the way they used to be, rich and great, both terrifying and voluptuous, the ones that are to be found only in past history'.[57] Regnault depicted this history in terms of a grotesquely violent execution inside the Al-Hambra; the title giving the painting all the historical validity it needs. A man has just been executed. His severed head lies on a step near the bottom of a stair-case. The executioner stands imposingly above, looking down indif-ferently at the severed head as he wipes the blood from his sword with his garment. The executioner's strong black body, bulging with tough muscles, contrasts sharply with the soft lines of his apricot tunic. The severed head has similar features and stature to those of the executioner – suggesting fratricide. The red of the blood, drip-ping from the body and pooled around the severed head, is diffused into shades of oranges and peaches as we look up to the executioner and the Arabesque background on which this scene of barbarity is being acted. There is no one in the picture to witness this act which is obviously committed in secret, without remorse or emotion, with technical efficiency and total ruthlessness – as befits the Orient. When the painting was exhibited in Musée du Luxembourg visitors were so overwhelmed by its reality they were seized by faintness; and, no doubt, their worst suspicions of the Orient were totally con-firmed.

Symbolically, the violent and barbaric Muslim male and the sensual, passive female, come together to represent the perfect Orient of Western perception: they fuse together to produce a con-crete image of sexuality and despotism and thus inferiority. The opposing principles generate expectations of the Orient that never failed to be fulfilled giving internal momentum to images so rooted in distorted desires and imagination. *The Slave Market, Constan-tinople* (1838), by the Scottish Orientalist Sir William Allen, com-bines the idea of an Orient made up of two opposing principles. Underneath the domes and minarets of the Blue Mosque, a family is being sold in slavery. The members of the family are being cruelly separated. The man has been sold to a Circassian warrior on horse-back and is being dragged off into darkness and a life of violence and barbarity. The woman goes in the opposite direction to the

harem. A number of people watch this transaction unconcerned at
the drama that is taking place. In the foreground, two Ottomans sit
deep in conversation unmoved by the cruelty before them.

Circles within circles

Orientalists' paintings show the Arabs as a race apart. Nineteenth-
century scholars incorporated this notion of racism and the innate
sense of progress of the Enlightenment in their philosophy. Spencer
and Comte 'scientized' this notion of racism to produce developmental stages of social life; Darwin 'biologized' their ideas and
unwittingly laid the foundation of Social Darwinism which become
a whole new stance on humanity and history. The concept of race,
which was also viewed in a developmental sequence from lowest to
highest, came to play a more overt part in judgements on social history. What those judgements consisted of was very old and familiar.
Hegel (1770–1831) set the tone. The central idea in Hegelian
thought is development. In history it appears as an evolutionary
process moving history through periods and civilizations towards a
progressive self-realization of reason. In the Hegelian scheme, history developed through four stages: the Oriental world, the Greek
world, the Roman world and, finally, the goal of the evolutionary
march of humanity, the German world in which Hegel himself
lived. Hegel considered the German world to be the epitome of
civilization because it gave full reign to reason by making freedom
a cornerstone of the state. In his scheme, Islam was of the Oriental
world and its sole purpose was to be a stepping stone to humanity's
ultimate realization, the creation of the German world. For him
Islam signified 'the worship of one, the absolute object of attraction
and devotion'.[58] But Islam's devotion to One was much too
abstract, too excessive; indeed, it excluded an interest in the human
world. This is why Muslim mood swung like a pendulum from
fanatic zeal to desperation, from one extreme to another. Because
of these extremes, Islamic civilization was self-destructive and on
the verge of writing itself out of history. Islam now had nothing to
offer except fanaticism, sexual enjoyment and despotism. Europe's
destiny lay in swallowing the antithesis of Islam into a new thesis of
its own. Hegel was simply spelling out Western anxieties and fears
about Islam: in the dreamland of European destiny, Islam looms as
a nightmare.

Where Hegel led, other philosophers followed. In his monumental work, *Weltgeschichte* (1881–88), L. von Ranke declared Islam to be an antithesis of Christian Europe. Jacob Burckhardt concurred. Ernest Renan declared that Muslims were the first victims of Islam. They must break the hold that Islam has over them, just like Europe had broken the chains of religious tyranny. But Renan was not sure that Muslims, whatever their history, had the capability of measuring up to the norms established by the European civilization. The reasons for this lie behind race – the moving spirit behind history. Islam and Christianity were not only two different religions, they were products of two different races: the genius of Christianity was the genius of the Aryan race, and the fanaticism and decadence of Islam rested squarely on the Semitic race. The Oriental mind, Renan declared in a lecture on 'Islam and science', borrowing the idea from Voltaire, is incapable of rational thought and philosophy and was responsible for blocking the development of science and learning in the Muslim world. The little science and philosophy that Muslims had produced was the result of a rebellion against Islam. The view that Muslims had produced no original science, but were only a conveyor belt for transferring Greek learning to Europe, became the orthodoxy until the middle of the twentieth century. Marx accepted Hegel's idea that history is a process, a man-made process, which could be controlled and modified. For him, history is the arena of human struggle and liberation as well as of promise and salvation. History acquires meaning in the future when salvation comes, not through divine grace, but through collective human action. Thus, Marxism, a Judaeo-Christian heresy, replaced religious eschatology with historical materialism. But the liberation and salvation of the Orient required first its destruction. Drawing from Adam Smith and Mill, Marx and Engels made a typological distinction between Western and Oriental history. Their argument was based on the climate and agricultural practices of the Orient. The mode of production in the Orient, they argued, rested on agriculture that in arid zones had to be carried out with huge irrigation schemes which had to be state-financed and controlled. It is not surprising, then, that governments in the Orient tended to be too powerful and despotic. Islam provided a typical example. Thus, the liberation of the Orient required destruction of its mode of production; and England was right to colonize India, where it had a double mission: 'one destructive, the other regenerating – the annihilation of the Asiatic society and the laying of the material foundation of Western society in Asia'.[59] As it turned out, both processes were totally destructive; and for Marx the Orient was nothing more than so much human fodder standing between him and the realization of his messianic vision.

A voice of sanity was supplied by the Konigsberg historian Hans Prutz. In his history of the Crusades, *Kulturgeschichte der Kreuzzuge* (1883), Prutz argued that not only had the West acquired the use of its rational faculties from Islam but also it was through contacts with the Muslim world that Europe learned to liberate itself from the suffocating embrace of the Church. As before, a furore followed and Prutz's voice was drowned in all the noise. A year later Gustav le Bon, in *La Civilization des Arabes* (1884), showed that the European universities had been living off the intellectual efforts of Muslims for over five hundred years. But both Le Bon and Prutz were overshadowed by Oswald Spengler. In his classic study, *The Decline of the West*, Spengler classified human culture into three basic types: the classical, the Magian and the Faustian.[60] Here Islam fits in the middle as the best expression of the Magian type sharing its 'Magian life-feeling' with such other 'religious' cultures of the Orient as Judaism, early Christianity, ancient Chaldean society and Zoroastrianism. Magian cultures, Spengler argued, are intensely dualistic, split between soul and spirit and were fervently messianic. The individuals of the Magian cultures experience the world as a cavern and project this experience in their sacred architecture and buildings, such as Christian and pagan basillicas, Hellenic and Jewish temples, structures of Baal worship, Mazdian fire temples and mosques. The best expression of this sacred architecture, derived from the cavernous experience of the world, is the dome; and the first mosque was the Pantheon, as built by the Roman emperor Hadrian! So the only thing that the Muslims could claim to be authentically Islamic dissolved into the dim and distant past of ancient history! Spengler is totally wrong on almost every count. His data has been shown to be spurious and he has been demolished by a host of scholars. The Muslim scholar, Muhammad Iqbal, known as 'the philosopher of the East', declared that 'his ignorance of Muslim thought on the question of time, as well as the way in which the "I", as a free autonomous center of experience, has found a place in the religious experience of Islam, is simply appalling'.[61] Despite that, just as most philosophers of history are, one way or another, children of Hegel, the influence of Spengler simply refuses to go away. But it is not just philosophers of history, such as Toynbee, Mumford, Sorokin and Suzuki, who are Spenglerian through and through, but even politicians such as Nixon and policy-makers such as Kissinger have found Spengler rewarding for understanding contemporary realities. However, it is Arnold Toynbee who imbibed Spengler more than most. In *A Study of History*, Toynbee identified twenty-one civilizations as constituting the totality of human cultures.[62] Borrowing freely from Ibn Khaldun, Toynbee argued that each civilization passes through three phases. The genesis always appears in religion which is soon institutionalized into a 'universal church' and leads to the creation of a 'universal state'. The state collapses when its centre of culture is attacked by outside barbarians. In the case of Islam, the universal church is the *ummah*, the global Muslim community, and the universal state is the Abbasid caliphate. The role of the barbarians here is played by Turkish and Mongol hordes of Central Asia, the Berbers of North Africa and the Arab nomads of Arabia. Toynbee also argued that the Muslim civilization consists of two distinctively separate societies: 'the Arabic' and 'the Iranic'. As to the 'fundamental question' of the 'parent society' of which the Abbasid caliphate is the 'final stage', Toynbee identified it as the ancient society of Syria. Seen in this light, Islam is reduced to a mere response to Hellenism; and Toynbee is able to locate the origins of Islam in the dim and distant horizons of the 'Syriac' society – almost fifteen centuries earlier!

To whisk through so many centuries of the history of the West is to truncate its complexity. But in our identification of repeated patterns of recurrences, it is not the Orient and Western acquaintance with the Orient that has been truncated. More detail of repetition of the same interpretation, the conformity of opinion and animus, could have been brought forward for each and every age and each and every Orient. But the detail would add little to the concluding point: underlying the complexity of the history of the West there is a continuity of stance to a necessary construct that is called the Orient. The overriding opinions were set when information was most limited and as information expanded its meaning and effect for the internal purposes of the West changed, but continuity was the essential feature of the Orient. There was change in the way the Orient was deployed, change in what information gleaned from the 'reserved laboratory' was taken to imply about human nature, history and the proper means of conducting the business of living. But these were preoccupations *of* the Western self *for* the Western self, and only after that, by extension of the relations of dominance, a matter of any consequence (and the consequences were huge) to the peoples of the Orient. All the aspects of the stereotype appeared early, different aspects of this coherent picture were more prominent in particular fields of Western thought and endeavour at different periods; there was disassociation, one part of the stereotype of concern in literary and artistic genres, while other aspects dominate in other fields. There was no need for logic, or integration because the object, the Orient, was not considered; it was constructed for present utility in the operation and advancement of Western thought. There simply has never been a definite object that is the Orient; the Orient is merely a pattern book from which strands can be taken to fashion whatever suits the temper of the times in the West. What we have gathered from history is a glimpse of this pattern which constitutes a theory and its practice that can apply itself to any aspect of literature, art and ideas. This coherent, but constantly reworked, theory and practice has for the West the ring of normality and reason for all that it is fable, myth and purposeful recreation of the realities that exist to the East of the West. This is the theory and mode of operation that has been and is Orientalism.

Theory and Criticism

It is a large claim to suggest a definite beginning located in history. A discussion of what happened in the past is also an attempt at representing the past. The validity of the representation, the substantiation of the continuing relevance of a point of origin can only be found in the underlying coherence of practice today, as much as through all the yesterdays that have been represented. A number of highly significant elements came together to make Orientalism possible. But Orientalism is unthinkable until these disparate elements find a focus. The representation of the past coheres around the Western response to the origin of Islam and the expansion of Muslim civilization. From this point of origin the West acquired and developed a stance, a body of ideas and a means of operation to interpret, represent, construct, interact with and deploy the idea of the Orient. In formulating a response, the West learned more and developed more of its own self-image than it did of the specific Orient it constructed, the Orient of Islam. The West lived with the Orient of Islam, and its own Orientalist ideas, for 800 years before it had significant encounters with any other Orients. From the Battle of Tours where Charles Martel turned back Muslim advance into Europe in the eighth century to the preaching of the Crusades in 1096 is the early, and as I have shown, defining phase in which Orientalism begins. The major fluorescence of Orientalism occurred in the sustained period of 400 years that separate the preaching of First Crusade and Vasco da Gama's landfall at Calicut in India. Orientalist ideas were already old, deeply ingrained at the time when new Orients entered into the experience of the West. It is possible to see how the interrelationship and interaction of the West with a variety of Orients was moulded by the reflexes and ideas developed in the preceding 800 years.

Contemporaneous concerns in relations with the Orient of Islam impelled and shaped response to new Orients. The representation of the past has shown change, diversity and reformulation in Orientalist ideas. It has also shown that the Western construct of the Orient of Islam has been a force in effecting as much as it has been affected by these shifts of emphasis. To make sense of where Orientalism stands today and how argument about the concept of Orientalism operates, it is therefore expedient to concentrate, as we have done in representing the past, on the Orient of Islam. Presenting a history of Orientalism through the discussion of a finite set of texts in a linear development could be seen as representing Orientalism as a monolithic system. Such a representation would be essentialist, it would see Orientalism as a fixed, unchanging discourse. A simplistic, essentialist interpretation would not take into account the fact that Orientalism has adapted itself to various historic situations; it would tar all Orientalists with the same brush, accusing them all of demonizing Islam and Other cultures whatever their individual positions; it would ignore any sites of resistance both in the West and the non-West; and it would ultimately project Orientalism as an all-encompassing totality. It would be more fruitful to see Orientalism as a whole series of discourses, changing, adapting to historic, scholarly and literary trends, but interconnected by a coherent set of common features. The coherence and the common features appear most clearly in the central relations between the West and the Orient of Islam. As we shall see in Chapter 4, the West is still squirming on the coherent features of Orientalist ideas, and demonstrating that centuries of scholarship have not improved knowledge to a point that removes or overcomes the impasse to mutual understanding. From film to fiction, foreign policy to polemics, Islam is seen and evoked as 'a problem', an immovable obstacle between Western civilization as its destiny: globalization. This impasse is the idea of Orientalism as a theory and practice as it has become known, as it has operated and continues to operate in the West.

Resisting Orientalism

An essentialist representation of Orientalism is, of course, open to demonization in reverse. If we see Orientalism as a meta-narrative,

the Orientalists themselves can then be represented as a group of
wolves determined to tear apart the religion, culture and civilization of Islam. And Orientalism could easily be portrayed as an
arch conspiracy against Islam and, by extension, all non-Western
cultures. One of the earliest polemics against Orientalism did just
that. In *Islam and Orientalism* the popular Pakistani writer,
Maryam Jameelah, reviews the works of six Orientalists, and concludes that 'Orientalism is not a dispassionate, objective study of
Islam and its culture by the erudite faithful in the best tradition of
scholarship'. Rather, it is 'an organised conspiracy' based on social
Darwinism designed 'to incite our youth to revolt against their faith
and scorn the entire legacy of Islamic history and culture as obso-
lete'.[1] Not surprisingly, she presents Islam as the binary opposite of
her own perception of Orientalism: as unchanging, fixed in history
and obscurantist. An innately hostile Orientalism is pitted against a
puritan Islam inimical to the West in totality.

Fortunately, most Muslim and Arab critique of Orientalism was
on a much higher plane. In his classic study, *English-Speaking
Orientalists*, A. L. Tibawi offered a masterly dissection of the techniques and methodology of Orientalism. As a historian, Tibawi
choose to expose Orientalism on the basis of historic accuracy and
objectivity. He deliberately tackled 'living', rather than 'dead
Orientalist', to emphasize the continuity of the tradition. Many Orientalist studies on Islam, he wrote:

> are distinguished by erudition, but if one penetrates beneath the
> apparatus of the learned foot-notes and the array of sources one is
> bound to detect an alarming degree of speculation, guesswork, and
> passing of judgement, for which little or no concrete evidence is pro-
> duced. It is, of course, one thing to be skilful in deciphering documents
> in Arabic (or Persian or Turkish) and quite another to be able to inte-
> grate the material culled therefrom into an historical contribution in
> the accepted professional sense. History in general is one of the most
> vulnerable of disciplines to the invasion of people from outside; it is
> often assumed that anyone who wields a pen can write history. In
> Islamic sources, the linguistic, literary, and historical materials are so
> intertwined that scholars are prone to attempt too much and find
> themselves writing history, almost unconsciously, with scant qualifi-
> cation for the task.[2]

Whatever the position of the writer, Tibawi argued, there is an obligation to state Muslim beliefs and views in their 'entirety so fully

and clearly as to leave no room for complaint of misrepresentation'.[3] Once that is done, the authors have the right to take issue with these views and argue their own positions. What the Orientalists actually do, Tibawi asserted, is to state their own views as though they were facts and than draw inferences from them. For example, the Orientalists assert that the Qur'an is Muhammad's own composition. From this assertion far-reaching historical, theological, literary and linguistic judgements are drawn which by 'sheer repetition are elevated to the dignity of facts'. To prove the assertion that Muhammad wrote the Qur'an, the Orientalists must prove that a man who could not read or write sat down in the first half of the seventh century 'in his study to consult and "quote" previous authors for the composition of the work known as the Qur'an'. But without offering this proof, the Orientalists proceed to locate the 'origins' of Islam in the Judaeo-Christian heritage. Thus, in *The Life of Muhammad*, A. Guillaume asserts that Muhammed makes allusions to the Gospel; and Montgomery Watt in *Islam and the Integration of Society* suggests that early Muslim works are peppered with 'quotations from the Bible'. How is this possible, asserts Tibawi, 'when there was no Arabic Bible to "quote" from'?[4]

The earlier polemics against Islam were abusive and deliberately misrepresented Islam in order to subvert it. But the new scholarship, asserts Tibawi, aims to be more objective. The new technique is to rely on simplistic comparative methodology to expose the 'defects' of Islam. So whenever Christianity is compared with Islam, the exercise is 'almost always to the disadvantage of the latter'. Moreover, Orientalists arrogate the power of interpretation to themselves and have taken on the mantle of being the guardians of Muslim tradition. They define the tradition and they guard it. They advocate 'reform' but that reform is subject to their approval. On the one hand, Orientalists allege that Islam is too rigid and must admit change. However, when far-reaching changes are made to the application of Islamic law, for example, these same advocates of reform assert that the changes are undermining authentic Islamic tradition. Extreme change, often propagated by Westernized Muslims, is hailed. But 'genuinely native reformers, with substantial followings, are frequently branded as mere "reactionaries"'. Nor were those who chose a middle way, more or less like their predecessors in the golden age, accorded unqualified approval, because, we are told, 'they did not go far enough'. What change is necessary, and how it

is implemented, is surely a matter for the Muslim community, Tibawi
asserts. Change within Islam is based on two guiding principles: it
should be in accordance with the interests of the community (*masla-
hah*) and the principles of justice (*adl*). And it is the community, and
not the Orientalists, who must decide what is in its own interests.
Orientalist scholarship is also brought into the service of Western
foreign policy and imperialism. If the Arab states act against the
interest of the West, the Qur'an and the traditions of the Prophet are
used to show that their actions are against the spirit of Islam. The
works of classical Muslim scholars are distorted to demonstrate that
Arabs and Muslims cannot adjust to the modern world. For example,
even though such terms as 'Arab patriotism' and 'Arab nation' were
totally alien to ibn Khaldun, Orientalist interpretations of his work
are used to justify the 'alleged inferiority of the Arabs'. Indeed, all
variety of political creeds, from socialism to reactionary politics are
being read into ibn Khaldun. In discussing the problems of the
Middle East, and particularly Palestine, only 'social, religious, agricultural, industrial, biological' problems are analysed, the political
dimension of the problem is often omitted.

Tibawi's concise and razor sharp analysis lead to three basic conclusions:

1 Modern Orientalism, despite its academic advances, continues to
   rely substantially on the medieval images of Islam; 'it has only
   discarded old-fashioned clothes in favour of more modern attire.
   Illustrations of the persistence of the old ideas abound, not only
   concerning the Qur'an and Muhammad but also quite logically
   concerning Islamic theology, law, and history'.[5]
2 Orientalist scholarship lacks clear thinking, objective standards,
   and basic courtesy, tolerance, and moderation towards Muslim
   points of view. In most cases, the religious and political affiliation
   of the Orientalists gets the better of their scholarly judgements.
3 There is no concrete or conclusive proof in the voluminous
   output of Orientalist scholars on the origins of Islam that Islam
   borrowed from the Bible or the Jewish scriptures. In this regard,
   Orientalist assertions are unproved 'vague generalizations'; and
   Orientalist scholarship is little more than a learned process of
   producing 'speculative discourses on the obvious'.

Tibawi's condemnation of Orientalism is not wholesale. He
readily acknowledges the work of those Orientalist scholars who

have genuinely pushed the boundaries of historic knowledge. In his classical paper, 'Orientalism in crisis', Anouar Abdel-Malek, too begins with identifying the positive elements in Orientalist studies of Islam and Arabs. 'The study of ancient civilisations; the gathering of Arab manuscripts into European libraries; the compilation of catalogues of manuscripts; the publication of a number of important works'; and 'the editing of studies, often deficient and erroneous from the linguistic point of view, yet rigorous in their method' have all increased our understanding of the past.[6] But these aspects do not represent the 'dominant vision of traditional Orientalism' which, Abdel-Malek argues, is deeply embedded in assumption, postulates, and philosophical and historical concepts that undermine the alleged objectivity of Orientalist scholarship. The main objective of the Orientalists, according to Abdel-Malek, was to examine and open up the 'ground they were to occupy, and to penetrate the consciousness of the peoples, the better to ensure their subjection by the European powers'. This phenomenon, however, was not unique to Orientalism. It was:

> a constituent element of all social science in the European countries in the period of imperialist penetration and colonisation: Italian Orientalism under Mussolini; the psycho-political penetration exemplified by Lawrence and his school, and before that the relations between missionary circles, the military and the Orientalists (notably at the time of the Third Provincial Congress of Orientalists in Lyon, 1878).[7]

Abdel-Malek distinguished between 'traditional Orientalism' – consisting of 'an amalgam of academics, businessmen, military men and colonial functionaries, missionaries, publicists and adventurers' – and 'neo-Orientalism'.[8] Both groups treat the Orient and Orientals as an 'object' of study inscribed by Otherness. This object was considered passive, non-participant and 'endowed with an "historical" subjectivity that is above all non-active, non-autonomous, with no sovereignty over itself'.[9] Moreover, thematically the nations, people and cultures of the Orient were seen in essentialist terms, which translated into 'a characteristic ethnist typology'. This typology, which was often converted into racism, was 'based on a real specificity but detached from history, and thus conceived as intangible and essential'.[10] Thus, European man, from Greek antiquity onwards, becomes the measure of all men everywhere.

Like Tibawi before him, Abdel-Malek sought to expose the methodology of Orientalism. He identified four main components:

1 Orientalism focused on studying the past of the Oriental nations and cultures. By positing that the most brilliant periods of the Oriental countries were located firmly in history, they made decline of the Orient a natural and inevitable phenomenon.
2 The past of the Orient was studied in its cultural (linguistic and religious) aspects and divorced from any social evolution; thus Arabic, for example, was studied as though it was a dead language. 'It is', notes Abdel-Malek, 'as if one set out to write a commentary on the French language (the language of Martin du Gard, Sartre, Aragon) on the basis of a reading of the Chansons de geste, the English of Shaw or Russell by reference to Anglo-Saxon, or the Italian of Croce, Gramsci or Moravia through a reading of ecclesiastical Latin'.[11]
3 Such a reading of history made living or resurgent history appear only as 'a continuation of a great but limited past'. As such, the history of the Orient ceases to be a life-enhancing force and is reduced to mere exoticism.
4 The achievement of the Orient, their contributions to science and learning, were deliberately ignored or suppressed. On the whole, they were deemed to be of little or no value and denigrated. This ploy was used to attribute the 'backwardness' of the Orient to its unproductive history and the alleged unproductive nature of Oriental history was then projected as 'a specific constituent characteristic of the Oriental reality'. Colonialism was thus absolved from all guilt.

This methodology, Abdel-Malek argued further, was used in combination with a number of 'instruments' of research. The primary sources of research were all collected, confiscated and otherwise taken from the Orient and accumulated in the great European metropolises. The indigenous scholars were thus forced to study their own national and cultural history using only indirect sources. The secondary sources on which the Orientalists rely so heavily – consisting of reports of colonial administrators, religious missions, as well as the accounts and reports of the managing boards of societies, travelogues and literary fabrications – 'are profoundly tainted with ethnism and racism in all its variants', the least extreme being paternalistic and drenched in exoticism.[12] Such sources, asserts Abdel-Malek, cannot and do not provide us with solid and objective research.

In contrast to Abdel-Malek, Syed Hussein Alatas offered a socio-logical analysis of Orientalism. His focus was the notion of the 'lazy native' which was the most common description of the people of Malaysia, Indonesia and the Philippines. Colonial administrators, who also tended to be scholars, and travellers to Southeast Asia were unanimous in seeing the 'leading characteristics' of the people of the region as 'a disinclination to work'. Alatas's painstaking scholarship analysed how, from the sixteenth to the twentieth century, the native was represented as indolent and offered a socio- · logical explanation for the emergence and persistence of the myth. One writer who contributed more than any other in framing an Orientalist representation of the Malays was Frank Swettenham. Swettenham, who was also the British Resident in Malaya, con-sidered the Malays, as Muslims, to be fatalist and superstitious. He suggested that they respected 'constituted authority', were 'good imitative learners' and could even be persuaded to accept 'inno-vation'; and rejected the common notion that the Malay was treach-erous: 'I question whether he deserves the reproach more than other men'. But his sociological and historical work had convinced him that the Malays were just not interested in physical or mental work. 'Whatever the cause', Swettenham wrote, 'the Malay of the Peninsula was, and is unquestionably opposed to steady continuous work'. Moreover, the Malays had no initiative whatsoever; they simply did what they were told by their rulers: 'They never thought whether anything was right or wrong, advantageous to them per-sonally or otherwise; it was simply, "What is the Raja's order?" '[13] If the Malays did not work, asks Alatas, how did they survive?

Most of the Malays, as well as the Javanese and the Filipinos, worked hard, every day and regularly. They toiled on the farms, planting, cropping, fishing, building houses and doing a thousand other chores of rural life. So how did the image of the lazy native emerge? Alatas suggests that this work was invisible to the colonist. A major factor in the Malays' reputation as indolent was their sheer independence. As the Malays were predominantly rural, their contact with the European colonists was somewhat limited:

The Europeans there had very little experience of Malays serving them. The Malays were not their pillars of comfort. In the bars, in the rest houses, in the hotels, in the shops, Malays did not serve the Europeans. The most which they did was driving and gardening. Malays were also not involved in construction labour, in road building, in clerical estate work, in short in the modern private capitalist sector of the economy.

Colonial capitalism, as thorough going system, was not confined to strictly economic areas. It embraced the entire system of administration, the school, and all other connected activities. Thus if the government built a railway, those labourers building the railway, and those running it, entered the network of colonial capitalism. The Malays entered this network indirectly in the civil service. They served a state administration manipulated by colonial capitalism. Since this did not bring the Malays into direct and regular contact with the European colonial community, their services were not appreciated. The Malays did not function in the total life pattern of colonial capitalism.[14]

The Chinese, on the other hand, worked to provide the Europeans with almost all their comforts. They worked as butlers, barmen, built railways, and ran small businesses that provided the Europeans with their 'profusion of luxuries'. It was thus necessary to generate a different set of myths about the Chinese: 'they smoke opium, they lie without restraint, and whenever opportunity offers are dishonest, cunning, and treacherous'.[15] But despite all this, the Chinese were seen as industrious simply because they supplied the lowest form of labour. The Indian had a similar status for the same reasons. Both Chinese and the Indians, because of their immigrant status, were compelled to work as slave labour, trapped in the worst type of mining and estate labour that Alatas describes in considerable detail. The Malays were considered lazy, not because they were really indolent, but because they could resist, and stubbornly resisted, becoming an integral part of colonial capitalism. 'Here was the sociological and ideological origin of the image of the indolent Malays.'[16]

The Myth of the Lazy Native was a groundbreaking work that had a profound influence on the scholarship of Orientalism. It offered the first sociological analysis of Orientalism. Hichem Djait's *Europe and Islam*, published in French a year after Alatas's study, presented the first philosophical interpretation. Djait suggested, rather paradoxically, that 'the uniqueness' of Europe's history made it 'incommensurable with (or opposite to) all other societies'. A comparative study of religions or civilizations could hardly be justified under this condition as Islam had become a problem for Europe by definition. And it constituted a bigger problem than all other non-Western civilizations. While China, for example, represents absolute Otherness, Islam has a number of things in common with Europe; indeed, it was 'one of the root causes' of Europe's 'rise to eminence'. The central problem that Europe has with Islam is that Islam played a predominant part in the ascent of Europe, it provided it with a basis for intellectual, scientific and technological development, 'suffered from and paid for its expansion and, finally, survived to defy the modernity it brought forth'.

Djait's work is much more than simply an insightful survey of Orientalist thought and scholarship – focusing particularly on French Orientalism. He saw Orientalism as a handmaiden to modernity and used Orientalism to offer a powerful critique of modernity. He was also concerned with both, breaking the spell that Orientalism exercises on the Muslim mind and liberating the West from the narrow confines of the Orientalist lore. The emergence of modernity has both left the problem of Orientalism behind and posed it anew. Orientalism does not ask Muslims to Westernize their souls; rather it now insists that they rationalize and modernize their lives. But modernity has also fragmented Western civilizations. Djait writes:

> Western culture was bound up with moral values as much as with a certain fundamental aspiration. Both of these, however, have managed to change their content while protecting their overall purpose. The civilization of the West was its way of envisaging life as a whole, its attempt to conquer nature, its endeavour to build, in the cities and the countryside, a particular human existence, and to provide an orientation for human activity. Up until the Industrial Revolution there was a culture and a civilization, and nothing more. Later, and until recently, these two structures succeeded in dominating the nascent power of technology, civilization by harnessing it, culture by simply ignoring it. But the invasion of technological modernity has broken the rhythms of the one and drained the substance of the other. The malaise of the West arises from the fact that it can save neither its culture nor its civilization, because of modernist logic. If the West desired to move boldly and bring about this sort of separation, it would not be able to, precisely because of the long and deep influence that industrialization has had on civilization, as well as because, more significantly, technological thinking itself derives, even though indirectly, from a fundamental cultural choice in favour of rationality. The

renewed stress on regionalism, the impassioned questions raised
about the anguish of modern times, the proliferation of sects, the culture of marginality, the rediscovery of communitarian values – all
these reactions testify confusedly to the same malaise over the rising
tide of inhumanity. And this response comes just when everywhere
else one sees at once the longing for that modernity and the extreme
difficulty of getting it.[17]

In Djait's analysis, modernity becomes an extension of Orientalism.
Modernity's attempts to bring non-Western cultures into the ambit
of its own notion of humanity is both a continuation of the project
of Orientalism and a reflection of the crisis in Western consciousness. Like Orientalism, modernity enables Homo Occidentalis to
continue to act out his Promethean vision: through modernity 'he
forces his rhythm and his choices on others, under pain of subjection or historical death'. Modernity ignores real history, its
struggles, its violence and its demands. It has incited the non-Western world to fight the West with its own weapons and drown itself
in a raving for development. It is foolish to assume, Djait wrote two
decades before Samuel Huntington recycled the thesis, that we are
heading towards a confrontation of civilizations. Rather, the threat
to all cultures and civilization comes from an instrumental modernity. 'And if there is any sort of solidarity that can provide a basis
for a truly universal aspiration, it is surely the solidarity of cultures,
including that of the West, against the enemy that denies them all:
uncontrolled modernity. Within this framework Islam can send
home its sublime message.'[18]

The Muslim response to Orientalism, and resistance to Europe,
can now take a more positive turn. Muslim intellectuals need to
understand Western civilization from within, 'to question it about
its essential nature, to explore its contours with both sympathetic
commitment and critical detachment'. This becomes particularly
pertinent at a time when Western civilization, Djait wrote with
brilliant insight, is simultaneously becoming insular and rethinking
its origins as is so evident from its politics. This 'auto-reflection',
argues Djait, 'is symptomatic of doubt and disarray. It could be the
prelude to a desperate kind of self-glorification. In any case,
Europe can no longer ignore the world outside or the modesty of
its origins'. But Islam too cannot ignore the 'inner drive' of the
West or perceive itself in 'monolithic and mythical terms'. Islam
needs to be more confident about itself for it is quite evident that

neither the Western civilization nor Marxism are capable of draining its cultural foundations. Thus, historical and critical thought within Islam can get a new grip on the whole situation. 'The Islamic intelligentsia can look at normative Islam from a certain remove, demythologizing its past without the nervous rigidity of self-accusation.' The role of Muslim intellectuals is thus not to put Europe's record or rationality on trial but to 'expose the whole range of European experience, in depth, to other norms, other values, and perhaps other categories. This is the way to hammer out a universal that will not be utopian nor destructive but the outcome of creative synthesis'.[19]

Muslim resistance to Orientalism must maintain a sense of rationality and a sense of history. The Muslims must accept, however false it may be in absolute terms, that they are 'backward'. But what does this 'backwardness' actually mean? 'It means that one fine day the West broke away from the pack of its fellows, running ahead, exhausting both itself and them. But in this unsporting race, with its peculiar rules, the one who jumps out ahead stifles his adversary, and those who fall behind are crushed.' The backwardness of Muslims 'is the dark side of the breathless race run by the West, which has chosen the pace, the terrain, and the goal'. However, because this 'backwardness' really exists, it makes modernity all the more tempting and catching up with the West that much more necessary. But since this gap is impossible to bridge, it is even more important for Islam to preserve its other values: an identity, a culture, a civilization. In other words: Islam 'should safeguard, cultivate, and refine its share, which is great, in the human enterprise'.[20]

Edward Said and his critics

Before the publication of *Orientalism*, Edward Said's much cited and contested study, critiques of Orientalism were confined to disciplinary boundaries such as Islamic studies, linguistics, anthropology, sociology, history and philosophy of history. Said, a Palestinian/American scholar, intellectual and activist, borrowed and built upon the earlier studies of Tibawi, Alatas, Abdel-Malek, Djait and others such as Abdullah Laroui, Talal Asad, K.M. Panikkar and Ramila Thapar; but he did not acknowledge any of them. Indeed, *Orientalism* seems to have emerged ready-made and fully-fledged, as though from nowhere, and proceeded to shape and dominate the debate.

What are the differences between *Orientalism* and previous works? Aijaz Ahmad identifies Said's treatment of French Orientalists, such as Chateaubriand, Nerval and Flaubert, and his use of the Foucauldian discursive theory as unique features of *Orientalism*.[21] Yet, in comparison to Djait's insightful analysis of French Orientalists, Said's treatment is easily forgettable. Moreover, long before both Foucault and Said became fashionable, Marshall Hodgson had argued, in a dazzling series of essays published between 1940 and 1960, that Orientalism, as a discipline and discourse of power, perpetuated the dominance of the West over the non-West.[22] The Orientalist outlook, Hodgson had suggested, was rooted in the Western notion of world history; and both Orientalism and Western civilization are based on the assumption that civilizations have essences and that these essences are to be found in the Great Books they have produced. Hodgson argued that the Great Books approach reduces history to a farce, obliterates change and presents the past in dramatic forms: as tragedy, in the case of Muslim civilization, or triumph, in the case of Western society. Thus we get the history of the West as a story of freedom and rationality and the history of the East ('pick an East, any East'), as a story of despotism and cultural stagnation. The idea of civilization as a discrete regional entity, Hodgson argued further, was quite meaningless. Muslim civilization, for example, is not limited to the Middle East or Asia. Its global nature makes it difficult for it to be studied as a discrete, regional entity. Islam broke many regional and civilizational barriers producing numerous new social and cultural hybrid forms which while undeniably Islamic were also unquestionably Arab, Indian, Chinese, Turkish and African. Only when Islam is studied as a global phenomenon does its history make sense. In the three-volume *Venture of Islam*, his best-known work, Hodgson showed what world history looks like when studied from an Islamic perspective.[23] Suddenly, Muslim civilization does not appear as a truncated version of the West but as a maker of global history on its own terms. Hodgson did not use the language of Foucauldian discursive theory but he presents Orientalism as a grand narrative that was used not just to misrepresent Islam but to make the history of Islam a small tributary in the grand universal history of Western, secular civilization.

So, is *Orientalism* saying anything new? Said is certainly not raising any new questions; neither is he providing a critique more profound or more thorough than his predecessors. As James Clifford noted, 'in the French context, the kinds of critical questions posed by Said have been familiar since the Algerian war and may be found strongly expressed well before 1950'.[24] In Britain, through a steady stream of books and papers, Norman Daniel and R.W. Southern had produced a consolidated picture of the origins, development and persistence of the Western images of Islam. On purely scholarly terms, Said's contribution is not very significant when compared to Hodgson, Daniel and Southern on the one hand, and Tibawi, Alatas and Djait on the other. Nevertheless, Said's book did start a new debate focused specifically on something called 'the Orient'. So what is this new debate based upon?

The new debate is based on three innovative features of *Orientalism*. First, to the standard scholarly and historical analysis, Said added a new dimension: literary criticism. To Arabists like Ockley and Gibb, colonial administrators like Cromer and Curzon, travellers like Burton and Doughty, historians like Muir, and Frenchmen such as Volney and Chateaubriand, Said added a new category: the values that enabled empire and imperial exploitation, he argued, also shaped not just the fiction of writers like Kipling, Forster and Conrad but the novels of even those figures we rarely associate with imperialism, such as Austen, Dickens, Hardy and Henry James. Indeed, Said contends, there would have been no European novel without imperialism. Second, Said was able to bring the different strands of critiques under a single interdisciplinary framework which transformed disciplinary critiques of Orientalism into multidisciplinary cultural analysis. Third, by using the language of Foucauldian discursive theory and literary criticism, Said was able to place the repackaged critiques of Orientalism into a new strategic location. It was this location, and Said's representation of Orientalism as the 'grandest of all narratives', an all-encompassing discourse that both represented and contained the Orient, that are the key to the success of *Orientalism*. Of course, Said's own location in the metropolitan academy of the West, and the fashionable genre of literary criticism, were also important. In contrast, Tibawi was working in the relatively obscure field of Islamic studies; Alatas was located in Singapore and worked in sociology from the unfashionable Third World perspective; Djait wrote in Arabic and lived in Tunis (although his work was translated, first into French and later into English); Hodgson was strictly a historian of world history; and Daniel and Southern were working essentially in European history. Paradoxically, the success of *Orientalism* is based on the very dynamic that sustained Orientalism as an arch discourse in the first place!

In presenting Orientalism as a meta-discourse, Said was able to incorporate all previous definitions of Orientalism into his analysis. So, Said defined Orientalism as:

1 The classical tradition of studying a region by means of its languages and writings; thus anyone who teaches, researches or writes about the Orient is an Orientalist. It is in this form that Orientalism lives on through its doctrines and theses, with expert Orientalist as its main authority.
2 'A way of coming to terms with the Orient that is based on the Orient's special place in European Western experience.'[25]
3 An overarching style of thought, with a history going back to antiquity, based on an ontological and epistemological distinction made between the 'Orient' and 'the Occident'.
4 A 'western style for dominating, restructuring, and having authority over the Orient.'
5 'A library or archive of information commonly and, in some of its aspects, unanimously held. What bound the archive together was a family of ideas and a unifying set of values proven in various ways to be effective. These ideas explained the behaviour of the Orientals; they supplied the Orientals with a mentality, a genealogy, an atmosphere; most important, they allowed the Europeans to deal with and even to see Orientals as a phenomenon possessing regular characteristics.'[27]
6 A 'system of representations framed by a whole set of forces that brought the Orient into Western learning, Western consciousness, and later, Western Empire.'[28]
7 The western 'corporate institution' responsible for dealing with the Orient: describing it, containing it, controlling it, teaching and learning about it, making statements about it, authorizing views of it and ruling over it by these and other means.

Using these all-embracing but contradictory definitions, Said constructs Orientalism as a relatively unified discourse spanning the entire course of history from antiquity to contemporary times. The

book presents a genealogy of Orientalism in which the basic features of the discourse repeat themselves in different epochs of
human history. Said's most significant argument is that Orientalist
'texts can create not only knowledge but also the very reality they
appear to describe. In time such knowledge and reality produce a
tradition',[29] which then shapes all further learning about the Orient.
Moreover, this knowledge tradition is so integrated with structures
of economic and political power that it became handmaiden to
colonialism; indeed, it articulated the forces of colonial aspirations
and justified colonialism in advance. *Orientalism* tries to demonstrate both how Europe invented the fiction of the Orient and the
Orientals and how this representation was used as an instrument
for control and subjugation in colonialism. Such a sweeping and all-
embracing definition of Orientalism obviously contains many seeds
of contention. And *Orientalism* has received praise and derision in
equal measure.

Perhaps one should begin by stating the obvious. *Orientalism* is
not an anti-Western polemic nor is it pro-Islamic. Neither is Said
representing Orientalism as a conspiracy nor portraying the West
as evil. All of these have been suggested by otherwise quite
respectable writers. The defence of the practice of Orientalism as
well as of the West and imperialism that have come as a retort to
the book are also rather transparent. For example, the argument of
Bernard Lewis, a senior statesman of Zionist historiography, that
Orientalism is disinterested scholarship and thus above criticism is
just too weak and ludicrous to deserve serious attention. In the
essays collected in *Islam and the West*, many of which provide
excellent models of Said's critique, Lewis suggests that Orientalism
is a neutral, rather innocent, classical discipline, much too special-
ized to be amenable to criticism from the outside.[30] Moreover,
Orientalism has nothing to do with politics and power; there is no
connection between Orientalism and imperialism, between the rise
of Orientalist scholarship and the European acquisition of empires
in Asia and Africa, and between Orientalism and the image of
Islam as the darker side of Europe. Lewis also seemed to be
troubled by the interdisciplinary nature of Orientalism; quite
natural for a scholar with his own disciplinary territory to defend
and preserve. He thus questions Said's professional competence:
while someone like Tibawi may be qualified to take on Lewis, what
qualifications did Said have to stray on the intellectual patch called

Islamic studies? This flat-earth view of Orientalism is also shared
by Ernest Gellner. Gellner, who accused Said of 'facile inverse
colonialism', was a great believer both in the 'scientific' nature of
'social sciences' and in the Enlightenment project. It is thus hardly
surprising that he was troubled by the notion of Orientalism, which
he dismissed as an invented 'bogey'; Orientalists like Bernard
Lewis, for Gellner, offered a 'dispassionate analysis' of Islam and
other cultures. Gellner's objectivity was clearly deeply subjective
for he was always eager to project the good in imperialism. He
wrote in a review of Said's *Culture and Imperialism*:

> Mobility, egalitarianism and free choice of identity have better
> prospects in the modern world than they had in the past. Should there
> not, on the part of one who seems to value this free, individualist
> choice of identity, be at least some expression of gratitude towards the
> process which has made such a free choice so much easier – even if it
> also for a time engendered an initial disparity of power between early
> and later beneficiaries of modernity?[31]

Both Lewis and Gellner represent a body of critical stance on
Said that Richard Fox has described as 'an unreflective opposition,
who refuse to budge from the idea of a value-free scholarship,
which is as mythical as any epic tale from India'.[32]

There are, however, some very deep theoretical problems both
with *Orientalism* itself and Said's own position on the discourse. His
notion of the 'Orient' is both too limited and too general. It is
limited to the Middle East and suggests that it is unique both in the
way it is represented by the West and the kind of imperialist or
oppressive writing produced about it. As I have tried to show,
Orientalism was by no means limited to Islam and Muslims; it was
applied, with and without changes and modifications, equally force-
fully to all other Orients: Chinese, Indian, Southeast Asian and
others. But Said's Orient is also so broad that it transcends time and
history, disciplines and genres and, as such, it is limited both in its
analytical capability as well as explanatory power.

A common criticism of Said is that he has presented Orientalism
as an unchanging, monolithic, predominantly male-orientated discourse. In contrast, Orientalism itself expressed a whole range of
voices, Islamophobics as well as lovers of Islam, hegemonic move-
ments as well as counter-hegemonic endeavours, differentiated by
gender, ideology and sexual preference. Said's reduction of this

diversity and heterogeneity actually amounts to Occidentalism – a stereotyping in reverse. In *Orientalism: History, Theory and the Arts*, John MacKenzie takes it upon himself to unravel the true variety and changing character of Orientalism. After a detailed examination of Orientalist art, theatre, music design and architecture, MacKenzie concludes:

> the artistic record of imperial culture has in fact been one of constant change, instability, heterogeneity and sheer porousness. It is impossible to recognise either the 'essentialised, basically unchanging Self' or the freezing of 'the Other in a kind of basic objecthood'. The western arts in fact sought contamination at every turn, restlessly seeking renewal and reinvigoration through contacts with other traditions. And both Self and Other were locked into processes of mutual modification, sometimes slow but inexorable, sometimes running as fast as a recently unfrozen river . . . the 'oriental obsession' was a continuing and constantly changing phenomenon, repeatedly adapted to the needs of the age and the yearning for innovation. Time and again, composers discovered their most distinctive voice thorough the handling of exotica. These were not passing fads, nor were they mere embellishments which ultimately left western forms unchanged . . . the capacity for assimilation often obscured the graft, but the resulting artistic organism was unquestionably new and different from that which had avoided all such contacts with the Other.[33]

But is there a contradiction, let alone an irreconcilable disparity, in arguing that Orientalism was as diverse, heterogeneous and porous as described by MacKenzie but was also enveloped in a worldview that saw the Orient from an essentialist standpoint which suggested some kind of enduring Oriental reality? In Islam, for example, there is a single worldview based on the idea of *tawheed*, the notion of one, omnipotent, God, that has generated a whole array of different outlooks, traditions, customs and lifestyles. Surely, diversity and complexity do not exclude collective arrogance or a common Western location far and above the Orient? Just because, as MacKenzie states, 'Orientalism was endlessly protean, as often consumed by admiration and reverence as by denigration and depreciation'[34] does not mean that it cannot, at the same time, be obsessed with the Other in a manner that the Other found denigrating, even in its admiring form. A paedophile admires and reveres a child before he denigrates and depreciates it! MacKenzie's argument sets up an artificial duality based on either/or logic;

the complexity of Orientalism suggests that it could/can be both: a rich and diverse enterprise conducted within an arch narrative.

If, as Said maintains, Orientalism consists of nothing but representation which has little to do with the 'real Orient', how was it possible for this imaginary construction and its knowledge to be put in the service of real imperialism, colonial conquest, occupation and administration? Notes Young:

> This means that at a certain moment Orientalism as representation did have to encounter the 'actual' conditions of what was there, and that it showed itself effective at a material level as a form of power and control. How then can Said argue that the 'Orient' is just a representation, if he also wants to claim that 'Orientalism' provided the necessary knowledge for actual colonial conquest?[35]

Moreover, is all representation misrepresentation? If representation can have an essence of truth, as Said sometimes implies, then, as Dennis Porter asks, 'how can it be justified on the basis of a radical discourse theory which presupposes the impossibility of stepping outside of a given discursive formation by an act of will or consciousness?' This 'fundamental contradiction' remains unresolved in *Orientalism*, Porter believes, 'due to the incomparability of the thought of Said's two acknowledged *maîtres*, Foucault and Gramsci, of discourse theory and hegemonic theory'.[36] Hegemony involves some notion of historical process 'in concrete historical conjunctures, as an evolving sphere of superstructural conflict in which power relations are continually reasserted, challenged, modified' – a notion that is 'absent from Said's book'.[37] Said is thus:

> led to claim a continuity of representation between the Greece of Alexander the Great and the United States of President Jimmy Carter, a claim that seems to make nonsense of history at the same time as it invokes it with reference to imperial power/knowledge. Accordingly, one important reason why Said apparently cannot suggest the form alternatives to Orientalism might take in the present is that his use of discourse theory prevents him from seeing any evidence of such alternatives in the past. In fact because he does not reflect on the significance of hegemony as process, he ignores in both Western scholarly and creative writing all manifestations of counter-hegemonic thought . . . The consequence (of this) is serious. The failure to take account of such efforts and contributions not only opens Said to the charge of promoting Occidentalism, it also contributes to the perpetuation of that Orientalist thought he set out to demystify in the first place.[38]

Orientalism's failure, Said argues, has 'been a human as much as an intellectual one; for in having to take up a position of irreducible opposition to a region of the world it considered alien to its own, Orientalism failed to identify with human experience, failed also to see it as human experience'.[39] But the idea of 'human' that Said invokes is itself part and parcel of the very same tradition that fabricated Orientalism. Notes Young:

> It was produced from the very same culture that constructed not just anti-humanist Orientalism, but also, as Said himself points out, the racist ideology of the superiority of the 'White Man' whose rhetoric of Arnoldian 'high cultural humanism' was defined against the intellectual and cultural depravity of the colonies.[40]

Young suggests that Said is unwilling to address the complexity of his position; Aijaz Ahmad notes that Said embraces the ideal of humanist values 'precisely at the time when humanism-as-history has been rejected so unequivocally'.[41] Said's paradoxical relationship with Western humanistic tradition leads to some strange anomalies. In particular, notes Ahmad, it suggests that:

(a) there is a unified European/Western identity which is at the origin of history and has shaped this history through its thought and its texts;

(b) this seamless and unified history of European identity and thought runs from Ancient Greece up to the end of the nineteenth century and well into the twentieth, through a specific set of beliefs and values which remain essentially the same, only becoming more dense; and

(c) that this history is immanent in – and therefore available for reconstruction through – the canon of its great books. Said subscribes to the structure of this idealist metaphysic even though he obviously questions the greatness of some of those 'great' books. In other words, he duplicates all those procedures even as he debunks the very tradition from which he has borrowed them.[42]

An objection commonly raised against *Orientalism* is that it offers no alternative to the discourse it critiques. Indeed, Said sees no reason why there should be an alternative: 'the general, essentialist paradigms which constitute knowledge of "the Orient" also constitute "the Orient" as an object in the first place – to provide an alternative to Orientalism would be to accept the existence of the very thing in dispute'.[43] Said insists that the object (the Orient) cannot challenge the subject (the Orientalists) by developing alternative models. But, as Michael Richardson notes, 'since the object has no real existence, being only a conceptualisation of the subject's mind, it can never be a question of the former acting upon the latter'. The only way out of this impasse is for the subject to represent the object more faithfully. But how can this be achieved? By the representations concurring with Said's own understanding? 'By what right can Said stand as a representative of the Orient? He is consequently forced in to a position that relies on precisely the same discourse he is criticising'.[44] Thus, while Said gives lip service to such alternative discourses as feminism and subaltern studies, he actually has no use of these discourses.

An alternative to Orientalism is not possible for Said, I would argue, because for him there is no option beyond secular humanism and its high culture. For Said, there is only one culture: European high culture which somehow contains all the seeds of resistance and liberation. Said exhibits as much hatred for things non-Western as the Orientalists showed towards things oriental. In his books on Palestine, which even his strongest critics have praised, a distinct dislike for Islam and Islamic culture is more than evident; and Said is never too far from the classic troupe of Orientalism in his depiction of Muslims. In *The Politics of Dispossession*, for example, the believing Muslims are dismissed as 'traditional' – the very word has notions of inferiority – simple, emotional, conformists. The '58 million Egyptians', Said tells us, all fall 'back into simple patterns of Islamic conformity' and seek 'emotional comfort' from their religion.[45] That religion could have real meaning for people, that it can be just as rational as humanism, are totally alien notions for Said. Hence he retreats into the classical European depiction of the Oriental as a child-like entity driven purely by emotional needs. In Said's vision there is no place for alternatives and in his world there is no place for Islam or Muslims to exist by their own definition. While all Islam, for Said, is a figment of someone's imagination, 'acts of will and interpretation',[46] secular humanism emerges in his thought as something real and concrete that he employs with all the force of neo-colonialism.

This is why any notion of resistance is so conspicuously absent from *Orientalism*. The native recipient of this discourse is passive and mute – a point Said reiterates in 'Orientalism Reconsidered'.[47]

Neither does the West offer an internal resistance to the discourse of Orientalism. Thus, far from offering resistance to Eurocentrism, I would argue that Said's construction of Orientalism takes the project of secular and Eurocentric discourse towards a new trajectory. His secular critique is as much a 'style of thought' and as ontologically and epistemologically rooted as the distinction between 'the Orient' and 'the Occident' that Said describes as the major characteristic of Orientalism. Indeed, in direct parallel to 'the Orient' and 'the Occident', Said posits a new binary duality, 'secular world' and religious world – echoing Salman Rushdie's construction of 'the light of secularism' versus 'the darkness of religion'. 'The secular world – our world', he writes, provides us with a sense of history, human worth and a 'healthy scepticism' about 'various official idols venerated by culture'.[48] Religion, on the other hand, is based on superstitions, has no basis for thought nor can it explain anything 'except by consensus and appeals to authority'. Now, this is not just a specifically Enlightenment notion of religion, it is also an Orientalist construction of Islam – the idea of authority through consensus being a particularly Islamic one. Through this 'appeal to authority', Said suggests, human beings have suffered more violence, more conflicts and more oppression than anything else. Religious wars and conflicts are the main reasons for untold tragedies in history and in our time. This uncritical stand on religion is not only totally incorrect but also less than competent. In purely statistical terms, secular ideologies in the form of fascism, Marxism, Stalinism, Maoism, Pot Pholism, nationalism, instrumental rationality, modernity, development and other notions have produced a level of violence that is not just greater but several orders of magnitude above anything that religious conflict has and can manage. Said presents 'Islamic fundamentalism' as an ahistorical phenomenon and then generalizes Islam within its framework. His romantic association with Western high culture blinds him not just from seeing that Orientalism, like colonialism, fractured and dehumanized Western civilization itself – a point so eloquently argued by Djait – but also that humanism is intrinsic to the worldview of Islam. Indeed, as George Makdisi has shown so brilliantly, it has deep roots in Islam.[49] Humanism came to Europe from Islam in the twelfth century along with the vast corpus of Muslim scholarship. Not only does Said refuse to acknowledge this history, he never allows Islam – its worldview, its history, its enlightened scholars –

to speak for themselves but insists on presenting a grotesque parody of Islam of his own construction.

This brings us back to the question of 'intellectual competence' which Said values more than 'truth or freedom' for it is the 'new prize' acquired by postmodern intellectuals.[50] But Said's own treatment of Islam betrays a serious ignorance of Islamic history and spirituality, Islamic political theory and history of Islamic science and learning, not to mention the vast contemporary Muslim scholarship of resistance and alternatives. But there is more than simply incompetence at work here. The logical conclusion of the discourse of Orientalism as constructed by Said is that all professional scholarship, to use the words of Bruce Robbins, is 'inherently elite and undemocratic' and 'based on a denial of self-representation to the oppressed, making possible a monopoly of uncontested and degrading representations of them by authoritative, self-accredited professionals' in the service of dominant groups. Scholarly careers are made not just by representing those who cannot represent themselves but by 'keeping the unrepresented from representing themselves, substituting their own elite intellectual work for the voices of the oppressed even as they claim to represent those voices'.[51]

We have placed the most influential contemporary theory and definition of Orientalism within the Orientalist tradition itself. Does any theory or practice that can be called Orientalism still exist? Said's definition is just one among many definitions; and his attempts at formulating a theory of Orientalism will always be open to criticism. It presents its own selection and structure to the common features of an ongoing theory and practice that is continually being remade. It is the process of remaking which links the Middle Ages to the diversity of Orientalism that is at work and among us today as contemporary praxis.

The Contemporary Practice

In modern times it is conventional to see the medieval era as far removed from the world of contemporary secular and scientific thought. The reflex is an invention of the Enlightenment. Enlightenment thinkers were dependent on ideas that were essentially medieval, however unpopular that assessment may be.[1] The form of dependence is the most interesting point. To argue their way out of medieval modes of thought and belief, Enlightenment thinkers placed the aspects of the Western self they wished to distance from their sense of progress and reformulation into the pejorative construct they made of the Middle Ages. Similarly, they placed much they sort to argue with or about in the Orient in a specifically inferior location. Just as the Orient was a utility for the organization and operation of their thought, so too was their concept of the medieval. As a consequence the Middle Ages have continued to get a bad press in the annals of modernity, the epithet medieval is always condemnatory. But this separation is more apparent than real. Ways of thinking as well as pervasive images that were formulated in the Middle Ages have remained in the Western psyche and have been continuously drawn upon, reformulated and reworked into 'modern' scholarship. This is the essential thesis of this examination of Orientalism. The patterns that have been identified, the continuous interaction and therefore transmission of ideas from one era to another, make Orientalism complicit, an integral part of the history of ideas across the whole spectrum of Western scholarship.

The very concept of modernity needs and deploys elements and techniques of Orientalism to establish its supremacy. Indeed,

modernity can be examined as another application of the reifica-
tion of the West to the yardstick against which all Orients and
Indies are examined. Modernity, as a concept, is nothing more than
extrapolation and abstraction of certain specifics of the historic
process of Western development. This abstracted framework is
then used as the definition by which absences and lack of development are detected in the Orients and Indies. The change of terminology should not obscure the identity of the process that is under
way, though compartmentalization of scholarship and proliferation
of neologisms achieve precisely that end. As Marshall and Williams
note, 'many of the clichés of twentieth century journalism about
Hinduism as an obstacle to "development" started their life in the
eighteenth century'.[2] The same could be said for any other Orient.
The concepts of modernity and development are built out of
accepted elements of the West and used as a comparative device
with the Rest. In such comparisons the West is the only acceptable
model. When modernity is employed as an outward gaze of the
West, it uses new languages, the terminology and concepts of eco-
nomics, sociology and political science. But what it seeks to define
and achieve has an exact identity with the missionary and supremacist instincts that were part and parcel of all earlier stages and
phases of Western expansion and its physical and intellectual conquest of the Orient.

Orientalism in modern scholarship

Ideas about the Orient are a part of the movement of ideas in the
West. Orientalist scholarship keeps pace with the shifts and changes
of language. It moves towards study based on the agenda of
'improving' the Orient, making it 'modern'. This transformation
can clearly be seen in such works as W. Cantwell Smith's *Islam in
the Modern World*,[3] H.A.R. Gibb's *Modern Trends in Islam*[4] and
Philip K. Hitti's *Islam and the West*.[5] In these texts modernity is the
yardstick by which the Orient is measured; and the spirit of Eurocentrism is kept alive by the kind of questions the Orientalists raise.
The basis of Orientalism remains largely the same; but the manner
becomes mild and polite. The new thesis, in reality merely a
reformulation of the old, is that Islam is incompatible with the
modern world; the assertion is justified by attempts to prove the
intrinsic inferiority of Islam *vis-à-vis* modernity. To give their

arguments some validity, the Orientalists often had to present a
total inversion of reality. Or perhaps because of the assumptions
buried in their methods of identifying and describing, which were
laden with all the old Orientalist values, they could only see reality
upside down. So, we find W. Cantwell Smith describing the *Ikhwan
al Muslimun* (the Muslim Brotherhood) in Egypt as emotionally
retarded folk driven by 'the hatred, the frustration, vanity and
destructive fury of a people who for long have been prey to poverty,
impotence and fear'. The 'modern world is too much for them' and
they are a force not for solving 'problems but to intoxicate those
who can no longer abide the failure to solve them'.[6] The element of
truth in what is presented as an academic analysis is negligible, a
distillation of supposed fact that is more akin to slander. The
Muslim Brotherhood has included among its membership some of
the most respected Muslim scholars of our time: Syed Qutb, Abdul
Qadir Oudah, Mustafa al-Sabai and Abdul Aziz al-Badri – scholars
whose intellectual output makes Smith's own pale by comparison.
The rank-and-file members of the Brotherhood were – are – not
uneducated fools who had no understanding of the modern world,
but scientists, engineers, medical doctors, academics and professionals, who by virtue of their policies and programmes could
attract mass support. It is worth noting that Smith had nothing to
say about Nasser, who persecuted and executed Qutb and other
members of the Brotherhood; on the contrary, he regards Nasser's
policies as essential for the cause of Arab nationalism and secularism. To sustain their thesis that Islam was incompatible with the
modern world, the Orientalists had to rewrite much of Islamic history. This turned out to be a negative variant of Whig history; the
decline of Islam was blamed firmly on its alleged failure to modernize. Philip Hitti's works on these lines were standard texts in the
1950s and 1960s. In *Islam and the West* he presented the Prophet
Muhammad as an impostor and the Qur'an as a rather jumbled
document based on Christian, Jewish and heathen sources. In the
age-old tradition, he stated that Islam made no contribution to
mankind with the exception, of course, of the celebrated *Arabian
Nights*. Exotic splendour was not the outcome of creative industry
but opulent indulgence, conspicuous consumption by court society
spent on concubines, singing girls, a few minor discoveries in science; but on the whole, Islam promoted only ignorance and stifled
intellectual activity.

While secularists such as Smith and Hitti were more directly
trying to prove that Islam was irrelevant to the modern world and
that only secularism could save Muslims from certain oblivion,
Christian Orientalists like Kenneth Cragg and Norman Anderson
used the old chestnut, Christianity, to make the same point.
Somehow Christianity had modernized itself; and if Islam did not
follow suit, it would follow a certain route to oblivion. It has
become conventional wisdom in such circles that in the last four-
teen centuries, Europe moved towards the intellectual ferment that
produced the Reformation. The Islamic calendar has now reached
the 1400s so Islam is ripe for Reformation. The underlying thesis,
once again, is that there is only one model, one time-scale, and no
alternatives; all civilizations must follow the course that has been
set by the West. Kenneth Cragg, who devoted his entire career to
arguing that Islam is inferior to Christianity, argued that the only
way forward for Muslims is to Christianize Islam. Islam is inferior
to Christianity, the old priest argues, because:

1 It lacks the notion of redemption of evil and seeks instead its
  forcible containment or elimination.
2 By marring the distinction between the sacred and the profane,
  Islam becomes a political faith. In Christianity, God intervenes positively in the world of human sinfulness . . . Islam addresses itself to
  the community and does not address the individual as a proper
  'person'.
3 It is the evolving flexibility of commitment that has opened the door
  to doubt and sin in the West. This is the strength of Christianity.
  Islam, in contrast, leaves no room for doubters; here God cannot be
  interrogated and, as such, Islam is totally inappropriate to modernity. If, however, Islam can be Christianized in this respect, the
  mystery of doubt and sin would bring man much closer to God.
4 The Old Testament prophets by 'confronting to the end the tragedy
  of human evil' offer a true representation of what prophethood is all
  about. The Prophet of Islam was not of this temper. The teachings
  of the Qur'an must therefore be supplemented by the Christian
  message.[7]

Norman Anderson argued that Muslims are quite incapable of
loving God; the evidence is that 'loving' and 'lover' are not attributes of God according to Islam! The Qur'an is not a 'satisfying
revelation' of God; for that Muslims must turn to Jesus. Moreover,
the Muslims cannot know God: accepting the Qur'an as revelation

from God does not take the Muslims very far in appreciating revelation of God – again for that, Jesus is the answer.[8]

Apart from the fact that all this is errant supremacist nonsense, neither Cragg nor Anderson can appreciate the profoundly obvious point: Islam is not Christianity. To investigate Islam according to the topography of Christian theology and Christology are naked attempts to 'discover' merely absences, it can only verify the investigators' own assumptions. That Islam might be different and yet incorporate many similar notions to cherished Christian values in a different structure of ideas and concepts is a notion that has hardly been entertained and, therefore, seldom investigated by the Orientalist. That the different form and statement of ideas and concepts is no barrier to loving God and believing and relying entirely upon His mercy seems to be beyond the imagination of Western writers, yet it is the truth lived by Muslims for all that. In Christianity, God's mercy and redemptive grace are mediated through the incarnation of Christ; faith and grace are the moving axes of Christian thought. Central to Islam is the pervasiveness of God's mercy and forgiveness, but the access to God and location for the exercise of this mercy is in the person of each and every human individual. Every human being has a direct, immediate relationship to God. The writings of these modern Orientalists clearly demonstrate that greater mutual understanding has not been a notable item on the agenda of Western scholarship. Understanding Islam, or any other aspect of the Orient, within its own context, on its own terms is not, has not been, the objective.

The Orientalist scholarship of the 1950s and 1960s, as exemplified by Smith, Hitti and Cragg, do have certain redeeming features. One could, as indeed Muslims did, argue with these scholars, engage in pointing out their underlying assumptions, and thereby draw them into dialogue. At the beginning of the 1970s, however, all this changed as the old strain of Orientalism reappeared in blatantly naked forms.

The early 1970s saw a cultural awakening in Muslim societies; it was also the time of OPEC and the revolution in Iran. All of these events were seen as a direct challenge to the West and its domination. Suddenly, Islam had 'returned' in a 'militant' form; it had became 'radical' and 'resurgent', and there was a 'revival' of 'fundamentalism'. The fact that Islam was always there through the entire colonial period and so many 'development decades' was

quite irrelevant. The old spectre of the dangerous and unimaginable monolithic energy of Islam acquired a new lease of life as the
image of Muslim 'fanaticism' and 'irrationality' reawakened in the
Western mind. The idea that Muslims were seriously disturbed,
and that the roots of this disturbance were buried in their barbarian religion, as the Orientalists of yore had always maintained,
returned with a vengeance. Orientalism, an academic discipline
that was predominantly linguistic and historical, was now crossed
with modern political science and sociology to produce a new
variety of Orientalism.

The 1970s and the 1980s are undoubtedly the richest decades of
recent history for Orientalist texts; no other period in this century
has produced such a vast and sustained scholarly and popular
attack on Islam and the Muslim world. Patricia Crone and Michael
Cook's *Hagarism: the Making of the Islamic World*,[9] Michael
Cook's *Muhammad*[10] and Daniel Pipes's *In the Path of God: Islam
and Political Power*[11] are three of the most representative texts of
the period and provide us with the flavour of modern Orientalism.
Hagarism, based on a document called *Doctrina Iacobi* – which in
'all probability was written' in the seventh century by Jewish rabbis
– sets out on a wholesale demolition of Islam. It is highly reminiscent of all those 'Vedams' and 'shastahs' that appeared in the
eighteenth century to warrant particular interpretations of Hinduism. *Hagarism*'s basic thesis is that there is nothing Islamic about
Islam; Islam, in fact, is a barbarian conspiracy with Judaic roots.
Crone and Cook adopt Eurocentrism of the most extreme, purblind
kind, which assumes that not a single word written by Muslims can
be accepted as evidence. They take the warrant of Orientalism as
scholarship, the authority to determine and describe what is
authentic and real, to the point of logical absurdity: the only way to
know anything about Muslims is from those who were not Muslims.
This is the purest form of Orientalism: because Prophet Muhammad and his followers migrated from Makkah to Medina, it must
be based on the Jewish idea of exodus; because Muslims practise
circumcision and sacrifice, the rituals must be borrowed from the
Jews; and so forth. The triumphant conclusion of Crone and Cook
is that Islam is an amalgam of Jewish texts, theology and ritual tradition. But, apart from the dubious *Doctrina Iacobi*, what other historical evidence do Crone and Cook have for this thesis? The
answer: none. Everything is 'probable', there are reasons (always

unstated) 'to assume', and 'clues' to any 'reassertions' are almost totally insignificant. The arguments in *Hagarism* might be summarized as follows: as the Jews of the early period shivered in the cold, sneezed and caught flu, and as the early Muslims also shivered in the cold, occasionally sneezed and caught some kind of influenza, Muslims must originally be Jews. When confronted with the depth of ignorance of Crone and Cook, Leonard Binder found himself totally dumbfounded. There is 'no more outrageously antagonistic critique of Islam than that which calls itself Hagarism', he wrote; and continued:

> The consistent theme of the work is that Islam is deeply flawed both as a religion and a civilization. Virtually no conceivable aspect of Islam is left without direct or indirect critique. Hagarism is described as primitive (p. 12), pagan (p. 13), inconsistent (p. 15), parvenu (p. 16) and barbarian (p. 73). The Qur'an is described as 'frequently obscure and inconsequential in both language and content' (p. 18). The significance of Mecca is described as 'secondary' (p. 24). The traditional date of the Prophet's death, as well as the orthodox conception of the role of 'Umar and the historicity of Hasan and Husain are all doubted (pp. 28 *et passim*). Both Judaism and Islam are dominated by rabbinic legalism and the pharisaic spirit, but 'in Judaism the other side of the coin is messianic hope, in Islam it is Sufi resignation' (p. 34). The synthesis of Judaic values and Arab barbarism is described as 'conspiracy' (p. 77), which permitted the 'long term survival' of Hagarene doctrine and the 'consolidation of the conquest society'.[12]

There is thus nothing in Islam but total barrenness, 'ethical vacuum', intellectual austerity, uniformity, fanaticism and barbarism in all its religious, political and physical dimensions. Why on earth, asked Binder in total astonishment:

> does anyone believe in Islam? The appeal of Islam seems 'puzzling', write Crone and Cook, in what must be the most astonishing passage in this astonishing book. The answer they give is that, despite its numerous inadequacies, Islam has great appeal in 'the world of men in their families' (p. 147). 'The public order of Islamic society collapsed long ago . . . but the Muslim house contains its *qibla* within itself' (p. 148). Thus do Crone and Cook deny what most others see as the essential and persistent aspect of Islam, and declare its public and political aspects to be mere illusion. Islamic civilization is, then, absolute difference, a jumble of unrelated atomic particles with no ordered, structured form.[13]

In *Muhammad*, Michael Cook, co-author of *Hagarism*, sets out to recreate the seventeenth-century picture painted by Humphrey Prideaux in *The True Nature of the Impostor Fully Displayed in the Life of Mahomet*. Despite its title, only 13 pages are devoted to the life of Prophet Muhammad, the bulk is made up of the usual mixture of half-truths, distortions, straight fabrication and racism. Most of his material, Cook says, is not to be found in authentic sources: 'the elaborate narrative traditions drawn on here are not to be found in the Koran'. So where do they come from? Cook does not tell us. In the end we have a strange genealogical 'sacred history' which, not surprisingly, is 'by Biblical standards rather stereotyped'.[14]

While Crone and Cook deny the very existence of Islam, painting it as a Judaeo-Christian conspiracy, Daniel Pipes argues that the very existence of Muslims is a threat to the West. The main thesis of *In the Path of God* is that 'Islamic resurgence' is a product of the oil boom, its chief architects being Saudi Arabia and Libya, its main ally the Russians, and its ultimate goal nothing less then the total destruction of the West. It is a contemporary restatement of the 'present terror of the world' thesis of Francis Bacon. Thus we are told that the mere fact of being a Muslim has profound political consequences: if only Iranians were Buddhist, a religious leader would not have vanquished the Shah; if the Lebanon were entirely Christian, the civil war would not have occurred; were Israel's neighbours not Muslim, they would have accepted its establishment. All the images, words and invective of Orientalism come to the fore, wrapped in political colours and rabid racial superiority, and are then presented as scholarship. In the xenophobic discourse of Orientalism, the distinction between scholarship and invective is not always easy to make. Such assertions were also the staple material of a vast corpus of popular non-fiction journalistic literature on Islam that appeared in the 1970s and 1980s. A representative example is John Laffin's *The Dagger of Islam*[15] that sets out to warn the West of the inherently violent nature of Islam and the Muslim world. The 'demonic' character of Islam, according to Laffin, stems from the stultifying doctrines of the Qur'an itself. There is no such thing as a Muslim intellect, no ability on the part of Muslims to think in abstract terms, no practice of 'contemplation' as in the Christian tradition. Any discernible refinement in Muslim civilization comes not as a result of Islam but from people whom the Muslims have subjugated. The 'brutal' and 'coercive' nature of Islam, Laffin states, also comes from the 'vengeful' and 'violent' behaviour of the Prophet Muhammad himself. Muhammad was an unscrupulous opportunist for whom ends justified the means and whose cardinal crime was that he was political. And so on.

It was hardly surprising that this trend ended with Francis Fukayama's triumphant declaration of the 'end of history'.[16] This popular and slight text asserts the ultimate victory of the inherent values and agenda of the West as a work of progress. The precepts of Western liberal capitalism have become the only rational universal dispensation, to contend and argue against any of their essential elements is therefore irrational and against the logic of history. Samuel Huntington's equally popular and equally slight paper 'The Clash of Civilizations'[17] also accepts the victory of Western progress. This, however, does not exhaust the possibility for conflict and the most likely conflicts of the future will be between civilizations and will be generated by civilizations that are intrinsically antithetical to the West. The most favoured candidate to instigate such conflict, the future lurking 'terror of the world', is hardly a surprise. Huntington's pronouncement is that Islam, with its 'bloody borders', is poised to pounce on the West.

Brown sahib and the Orientalized Oriental

Most non-Western countries gained their independence from the late 1940s through to the early 1960s. This period also saw the emergence of a new variety of indigenous Orientalism located in a particular brand of scholar, writer and thinker. Described variously as 'captive minds', 'brown sahibs' and the 'Orientalized Orientals', this group of local Orientalists is defined by its acute state of intellectual bondage and total dependence on the West. A captive mind is not uncritical; it is critical only on behalf of the West. Nevzat Soguk has defined the 'Orientalized Oriental' as:

> one who physically resides in the 'East', and sometimes in the West, yet spiritually feeds on the West. S/he announces her/himself to be 'post-Oriental', or 'postcolonial', yet is a practicing member of the 'orientalising' praxis in its daily operations in the interpenetrating realms of art, aesthetics, folklore, media, education, and so on. S/he is the non-Western subject who makes her/himself largely in the image

of the West, its experiences, designs, and its expectations ... for her/him the 'West' is always more intelligible and fulfilling, and thus more attractive than the East.[18]

The Orientalized Orientals are a very specific Western creation, a product of over a century of conscious policy. We can trace the moment of their creation in Macaulay's famous Minute of (Indian) Education of 1835: 'we must at present do our best to form a class who may be interpreters between us and the millions whom we govern; a class of persons, Indian in blood and colour, but English in taste, in opinion, in morals, and in intellect'.[19] The first step towards this goal was to give, in the words of William Hunter, Director-General of the Statistical Department of India, writing in 1871, 'the educational system of the Musalman' a 'deathblow'. Thus Muslim institutions of learning were systematically uprooted and their products, who were among the leaders of those challenging British domination, were abused, ridiculed and identified as the prime cause of Muslim backwardness. What the British did in India, Malaysia, British Africa and the West Indies, the French did in the Maghrib and the rest of Francophone Africa, Asia and the West Indies, and the Dutch in Indonesia. In all cases the goal was the same: to rearrange, in the words of Vittachi, the 'neural intellectual circuitry' of the co-opted individuals 'in a colonial pattern' and to 'replace a clear white colonialism with a murky brown colonialism'.[20]

Thus, departing colonial powers left a not-so-departing legacy for the newly independent states: a dominant class of politicians, administrators, bureaucrats, writers and thinkers that identified strongly with colonial culture. The politicians and decision-makers who took over from the colonial powers – such as Jawaharlal Nehru, Aung Sang, Soloman Bandaranaike, Lee Kuan Yew, Tunku Abdul Rahman, Nkrumah and Kenyatta – were all deeply and broadly colonized in their minds. Their perpetual goal – to grasp European civilization – meant downgrading local history, literature and culture and identifying strongly with European history and cultural artifacts. They considered every element of indigenous culture to be backward and worthy only of being dumped onto the scrap heap of history. They often took particular pride in their ignorance of their own history and pleasure in parading their ignorance in public. When M.R. Singer studied the brown sahib in the early 1960s, he was surprised to note that for them 'the British parliament is the mother of democracy, and Hobbes, Burke, Locke and Hume were absolutely correct'; it was forgivable for a brown sahib not to know the basic facts about the Mughals, or anything about the great literary works of Urdu and Hindi, or even the basic tenets of Islam, but it was 'downright unthinkable for him not to know who signed the Magna Carta'.[21]

The colonial era, even in countries that were never formal colonies, established a complete separation between traditional and modern education. Modern education was education in disciplines formed and based exclusively on Western scholarship. Such education required students from the non-West to ingest the constructs of Orientalism inherent and complicit in all branches of Western thought and scholarship. The history and thought of the Orient was therefore learned as it had been determined, assessed and described from superior authority by the West. It is little surprise therefore that sociological and anthropological studies conducted by scholars of and from the non-West on their own community provide a seamless continuation of the scholarship of the West. A particularly apposite example is the Egyptian sociologist Saad Eddin Ibrahim[22] whose view of the rise of Muslim 'fundamentalism' in contemporary Egypt and its attraction for the uprooted population undergoing the shock of urban relocation is in essence exactly the same as Cantwell Smith's. There is a sense in which such scholars from the Orient create a new, self-fulfilling continuous feedback loop. Ibrahim was interviewed in Granada Television's documentary *The Sword of Islam*, one of the most comprehensive Orientalist texts of recent times. Its script accurately sets out the problems of modern Egypt, the familiar terrain of misdevelopment and the awful predicament they create. The authoritative voice of the programme then expresses incomprehension not just that Egyptians should wish to find an alternative to the failure inherent in modernity as they live it, but they could countenance that a religious revelation that is 1400 years old can be turned to for political and economic ideas for the modern world. Presenting Islam as a narrow theology of personal devotion and morality, it describes the mosques as 'sepulchres' – only dead bodies live in tombs! The warrant for such prejudice masquerading as fair comment is the explication of the Egyptian sociologist who in the terminology of alienation, disaffection with the problems of

modernity and the uprooting of the drift to urban centres essentially makes the case that Islam is incompatible with the modern
world. On this authority, spoken supposedly from within, it is then
permissible to deploy the Orientalist construction and direct the
gaze of the television camera towards the classical images. The programme begins with the most concentrated burst of Orientalist
imagery. A globe, our world, appears spinning in space, then a
curved scimitar appears, by convention an 'Islamic' sword. It whirls
and neatly cleaves the globe, which bursts apart in an explosion of
blood. After such an opening sequence, two hours of supposedly
detailed investigation is quite superfluous – the message was con-
veyed in the first 20 seconds. Where in the past it was possible to
see Orientalism as a process inflicted upon the Orient, today it
exists and operates within the Orient itself and creates a destabil-
izing ideological divide that has social, political and economic consequences. The effect of this Orientalism from within the Orient is
tension and contention in which the West appears to be a neutral,
non-participant observer that finds its own history and opinions
greatly enhanced and given greater authority by the opinions of
Orientalized Orientals.

V.S. Naipaul and Salman Rushdie are undoubtedly the most
notorious brown sahibs of recent times: the first grounded in modernity; the second a self-confessed 'postmodern writer'. Like most
brown sahibs, Naipaul takes every opportunity to boast of his ignorance of India, Islam and Muslims; Rushdie appeals to his 'special
knowledge' of his cultural background to shape a constructed
ignorance. Both seek to defend 'the light of secularism' against 'the
darkness of religion' taking every opportunity to paint Islam in the
classical colours of Orientalism in the process. Naipaul's *Among the
Believers: An Islamic Journey*[23] and Rushdie's *The Satanic Verses*[24]
have become the classic texts of modern and postmodern Orientalism. Naipaul begins his journey in Iran by admitting that he is
totally ignorant both of Iran and Islam. He had always known
Muslims, he says, but he knew nothing of their religion:

> The doctrine, or what I thought was its doctrine, didn't attract me. It
> didn't seem worth inquiring into; and over the years, in spite of travel,
> I had added little to the knowledge gathered in my Trinidad child-
> hood. The glories of this religion were in the remote past; it has gener-
> ated nothing like a Renaissance. Muslim countries, where not
> colonies, were despotisms; and nearly all, before oil, were poor.[25]

His knowledge of Iran is not much better either:

> I hadn't followed Iranian affairs closely; but it seems to me, going only
> by the graffiti of Iranians abroad, that religion had come late to Iran-
> ian protest. It was only when the revolution had started that I under-
> stood that it had a religious leader.[26]

This ignorance is all-pervasive, intrinsic and deeply rooted; it
cannot be cured by a dose of knowledge. Naipaul sets out, travels,
sees and comments with all the convictions and conventions of the
generations of Western travellers who went before. He is a latter
day Chardin, Bernier, and Montecroce out of Guibert of Nogens
and St Bernard all rolled into one. When his Communist guide suggested 'to understand I should go to the holy city of Qom and talk
to people on the streets', he declines not just because of his obvious
difficulty with the local language but more because he did not want
his prejudices shattered. His ignorance is multi-layered and
revealed on almost every occasion. For example, when he heard the
name of Avicenna, he exclaimed: 'Avicenna! To me only a name,
someone from the Middle ages: it had never occurred to me that he
was a Persian' which also reveals his ignorance of Chaucer who
invokes Avicenna in the Prologue to *The Canterbury Tales*.[27] He is
surprised to hear the Iranians talking about a constitution: 'They
might not have ideas about a constitution – a constitution was, after
all, a concept from outside the Muslim world'. But any contemporary text on constitutional history would have told him that the first
written constitution in the world is connected with the Medina state
of the Prophet Muhammad. A life based on the Qur'an, he wrote,
is simple: 'it has rules for everything; and everyone had to learn the
rules'. But, even a distorted translation of the Qur'an would have
shown him that the Qur'an has few rules; indeed, one-third of the
Qur'an is devoted to exhorting the believers to think, ponder,
reflect. Over dinner at the Holiday Inn in Kuala Lumpur, he is surprised to see a fashion show on a Friday. It is meant, he tells his
readers, for non-Muslims, or 'Muslims not observing the Sabbath'.
Obviously his childhood friends in Trinidad did not tell him that
Friday and Sabbath have no connection whatsoever. When he was
told that students at the seminaries in Qom study for six years, he
was amazed: 'What did they study all that time?' Naipaul's ignorance, however, is not limited to religion, history or current affairs,
but it extends even to methodology. In a market in Karachi he

picked up a copy of *Chachanama*, a book of fairy-tales similar to the *Arabian Nights* and a great favourite of school children. No journalist, no historian, no one with even a modicum of critical training, would consider *Chachanama* as an historical source; it is akin to trying to write the history of the Renaissance by talking to a taxi-driver. Yet, Naipaul relates the entire history of the Subcontinent, the arrival of Islam, various conquests, from this book of fairy-tales as though they were historical facts!

In Naipaul's modern world, things exist in two clear-cut categories: secularism is good, but Islam and anything to do with it is bad. He is full of praise for the 'despotism' of Zulfiqar Ali Bhutto, but bitter about General Zia's 'despotism' simply because Zia tried to justify his action in Islamic terms; military dictatorship in Pakistan is bad because Pakistan is an Islamic republic, but the military dictatorship in Indonesia is good because it is a secular republic. Acceptance of Islam as one's faith is giving in to the imperialism of Islam; acceptance of Western values and culture is the triumph of liberalism. Given the division of the world into black and white, it is no wonder Naipaul cannot understand why people educated in the West are 'converted' to Islam. Why are most Muslim activists to be found in the science and engineering faculties of the universities? These questions are too complex for Naipaul to understand, so he follows the well-chosen path of the ignorant: ridicule. Exactly the same process is repeated in *Beyond Belief: Islamic Excursions Among the Converted Peoples*[28] his second 'journey' into the Muslim world. The absurd thesis presented here is that if you are not an Arab you are, by definition, a convert to Islam – Islam being solely an Arab religion! So Pakistanis, Iranians, Malaysians and Indonesians can only be inauthentic Muslims cut off from their traditions and history; these folks are thus doomed to be forever unhappy, forever confused, forever inferior. The lionization of Naipaul, whose sympathies for 'authentic' Hindu fascism are well known, and whose ignorance and bigotry are almost fathomless, says a great deal about the Western literary establishment's boundless love for Orientalism.

Authenticity is, of course, an Orientalist trope. Only the Orientalists have the authority to determine what about Islam and the non-West is 'authentic' and 'inauthentic'; the Others are just too ignorant of their own history and tradition to know anything authentic of their past. Postmodernism shuns all notions of authenticity as well as those fundamental ideas that shaped modernity. The project of modernity, as Habermas has said, is to develop the sphere of science, morality, art and literature according to their inner logic. With its stress on the purity of each art and the autonomy of culture as a whole, postmodernism takes modernity to its logical conclusion. While it ostensibly seeks to demolish 'grand narratives' – reason, science, religion, tradition, Marxism etc. – postmodernism actually privileges a single grand narrative: liberal secularism. It is under the over-arching umbrella of bourgeois liberal secularism that all other imposing ideas and notions of truths are supposed to be equal. It is not surprising then that Rushdie's *The Satanic Verses* finds Islam inferior to secularism and thus tries to secularize and strip it of all its sacred content. Rushdie attempts this by rewriting the Seerah, the life of Prophet Muhammad, the paradigm of Muslim behaviour and identity, and seals it in his own, dogmatic secularist, image. *The Satanic Verses* is thus an exercise in undermining both the sacred history of Islam and the very personality that defines Muslims as Muslims and thus to erase the entire cultural and religious identity of Muslim people. Such an exercise could not be attempted without recycling the potent images of Orientalism; Rushdie relies on these images to such an extent that his fictionalized Muhammad is dubbed Mahound, the Devil's synonym from *chansons de geste*! Norman Daniel, who is the ultimate authority on medieval images of Islam, suggests in the revised edition of his classic 1960 study, *Islam and the West*, that an average reader from the Middle Ages will be perfectly at home with Rushdie's depiction of Islam and its Prophet. 'Enemies of Islam', Daniel writes, 'whatever their motives, will always exploit and distort much the same facts, as did recently Salman Rushdie's *Satanic Verses*; the style of the day changes, but the themes are perennial'.[29] No wonder the Muslims of all shades of opinion rose up in unison against the novel.

The Orientalized Oriental sees the culture of his/her origins, as the mirror of the West. The non-Western world exists to fulfil the Western Self: there are no non-Western humans or human relationships with the ideational or cultural reality of the Other. All civilization is Western civilization, all history is Western history. Cultures are packed in a hierarchical order: every culture is walking the incline plane of history, slightly out of breath, desperately trying to become like the culture of modernity, or be assimilated in postmodernism, the zenith of Western civilization. All societies are

marching towards a single utopia, the ultimate Western organizing
principle for society: secularism. *The Satanic Verses*, by appropriating the sacred territory of Islam and secularizing it, aims to reduced
Islam to an appendage of Western civilization, a segment of the
history of secularism. This is exactly the project we first encoun-
tered with the system builders of the Enlightenment. In *The Satanic
Verses* this feat is carried out with techniques that were the special-
ity of Enlightenment thinkers: parody and ridicule. Islam, the
worldview that gives meaning to the life of a quarter of mankind,
thus becomes superfluous. When ignorance, including constructed
ignorance, is combined with arrogance, a lethal amalgam is produced. The hatred of Islam that Rushdie and Naipaul demonstrate
in their works is a product of brown sahib programming that began
under colonialism. And as ideal colonial surrogates, the brown
sahibs fulfil the ultimate desires of their colonial masters by going
the distance that even the Western Orientalist would not go. In the
final analysis, they provide a confirmation of what the Orientalist
representation had always advocated: the inferiority and backwardness of Islam. This is why the noted Indian thinker Ashis
Nandy describes the works of Naipaul and Rushdie as 'inhuman
and ethnocidal'.[30]

Orientalism in popular fiction

The Satanic Verses is pure Orientalism aspiring to be art. Orientalism has always had a vibrant life in art and the diverse products of
popular culture, it is the medium through which scholarly ideas
have been spread until they are 'as thin as reality', an ubiquitous
presence everywhere repeated. A reader of contemporary popular
fiction can be forgiven for believing that Muslims are hell-bent on
destroying that bastion of democracy and freedom, the United
States. There is almost a direct parallel between American foreign
policy with its current designated demon – now the Palestinians,
now Colonel Qaddafi of Libya, now Imam Khomeini of Iran, now
Saddam Hussein of Iraq – and the villains of popular pot-boilers.
From John Updike's *The Coup*[31] to Phillip Caputo's *Horn of
Africa*[32] to John Randall's *The Jihad Ultimatum*[33] to Frederick
Forsyth's *The Fist of God*[34] the message is loud and clear. John Ran-
dall's *The Jihad Ultimatum* is a good example of the genre. A group
of Iranian terrorists arrive in New York, armed with an atom bomb

generously supplied by Colonal Qaddafi of Libya, with the aim of frightening the US into submission. Led by Zaid abu Khan, the terrorists of Islamic Jihad demand that huge amounts of aid, in the form of money, technology and weapons, should be given to Iran. The convoluted plot, involving endless double-crosses, the KGB, a deranged Gorbachev bent on world domination, the CIA, and a sophisticated US president, provides a backdrop for painting Muslims and Islam in all the colours of Orientalism. Virtually all Muslims in *The Jihad Ultimatum* are terrorists and inhuman individuals. Zaid abu Khan, the leader of the Iranian Jihad, is an evil killer motivated by revenge and an obsession with Islam. He wanders about in the book 'open-mouthed in rapture', uttering sentences such as 'America . . . will become ugly and uninhabitable – raped by the strength of the Jihad' and 'We will drive a stake of terror through their hearts . . . from sea to shining sea'. Khalid Rahman, Khan's number-two man, prefers action to politics: 'for him, there is only one cause, one leader, and that is Allah – although it appears as if Zaid abu Khan is now his representation of Allah'. Rahman is so stupid that he thinks that Khan embodies all the characteristics of the Prophet Muhammad. Bafq el-Rashid, the ammunitions expert, is a violent, evil man who rapes his colleagues, particularly al-As, to ensure that they remain subordinate to him. Al-As himself is 'a ruthless killer' and hence 'a leader of the future'. The Iranian president, Waquidi, is a total weakling whose policy is dictated by the terrorists. The US president describes him as 'a third-rate bureaucrat from a nation whose political and religious back-ground were more than foreign to him'. He has no understanding of the modern world; when US troops attack Tehran and capture him, he is found sitting in his room, babbling and amazed at the sights and sounds of the battle going on around him. Frederick Forsyth's *The Fist of God* turns the guns on Saddam Hussein. Cobbled together from newspaper cuttings, *The Fist of God* begins with the murder of a Canadian gun designer, Dr Gerald Bull, who had been in the process of developing a massive weapon known as the 'Supergun' for Iraq. Saddam Hussein is going to use the gun to launch an atomic bomb into orbit that would, at an appropriate time, re-enter the atmosphere and destroy the United States. The plot involves British intelligence agents penetrating Iraq dressed as Bedouin tribesman from the desert – à la Richard Burton and Charles Doughty – British Orientalists who know more about Arabs than the Arabs

themselves, and heroic British businessmen who are more interested in democracy than selling arms.

When Muslims are not out to destroy the United States, they
become comic figures that personify the inferiority of Islam. In
Michael Carson's *Friends and Infidels*,[35] for example, we have a
typical portrayal of Arabs as quite incapable of ruling themselves.
Indeed, the king and inhabitants of the comic state of Ras Al Surra
cannot do anything for themselves – they need those hardy peren-
nials, the British, to come and settle in their country to do all the
jobs 'that Ras Al Surrans are deemed incapable of doing'. Even the
names of their villages reflect their ignorance; the town where the
action takes place is called 'Jaheel', the Arabic word for dumb
ignorant! The notion of progress is quite alien to the folks of Ras
Al Surra and they have to learn about the importance of electri-
city, water supply and sanitation from the expatriates who 'will lift
all to a paradise of prosperity and ease'. This is, of course, the
Arabia of T.E. Lawrence: backward, inferior, but in Carson's hand,
quite funny and humane. But in other hands, this sort of thing
degenerates into pure racism. In Phillip Caputo's *Horn of Africa*,
for example, racism is more than skin deep as Caputo's sense of
racial superiority and 'civilization' jumps out of every page. We find
Cairo to be 'a fly plagued decaying mess' with taxi drivers 'cursing
as only Arabs can'. The language of the locals has 'that demeaning
invective for which Arabic seems to have been invented'. The
Palestinians are 'prepared to trample on every law and convention
in pursuit of their aim'; their creed is 'the romantic worship of violence, violence for its own sake'. The inhabitants of Jubaya, where
much of the action takes place, have the same light in their eyes as
the hero had seen in the eyes of Palestinian guerrillas, 'the gleam
of something darker than madness – belief, an absolute belief in the
rightness of one's religion or political dogma or personal destiny'.
Indeed, the eyes tell everything: 'I knew it from his shining eyes: he
was a fanatic'. The whole narrative is divided into two clear-cut div-
isions: the white characters, on the one hand, are civilized, polite,
humane and, even when they are committing acts of mass murder,
rational; the Muslims, on the other, are bloodthirsty, alien, barbaric
and savage. But the characterization and narrative are secondary
to the point of view of the author: Caputo's 'personal vision' of violence and of 'a certain kind of man' prone to such violence: the
Muslim.

Orientalism on film

The representation of Muslims as inherently violent and deranged characters is as pervasive in the vocabulary of Hollywood films as it is in pot-boiling novels. The cinema is, of course, the dominant medium of mass popular culture of the twentieth century. And we find on the silver screen all the age-old stereotypes recycled, revived, refreshed and reinvested. While these signifiers represent old ideas, their contemporary function is to keep the worldview of Sir John Mandeville to the forefront of Western consciousness, easily accessible and instantly familiar to new generations who could otherwise think the past remote and quite different from today. The representation of Muslims as evil terrorists is so deeply etched in Hollywood consciousness that they are now used as standard plot devices even in narratives that have no connection with the Orient whatsoever. The unseen terrorists in *Back to the Future* (1985) who set the story rolling are said to be 'Libyan'; the faceless men in the desert who serve as target practice for *G I Jane* (1998) speak Arabic; when brave white heroes want to perform their martial arts routines in American cod-Zen films, such as the various 'American Ninja' flicks, they are customarily presented with stock Arab villains to beat up. Today, the lurking menace of the fanatical Muslim performs the script function that the Red Menace of the American Indian once provided in that dominant genre of cinema entertainment, the Western. It is no longer politically correct or culturally sensitive to make that kind of Western anymore. Some of the Indies have been re-evaluated and remade. The Orient, however, has not undergone such a change. *Lives of the Bengal Lancers* (1935), a standard Hollywood depiction of the British in India, is structurally an Eastern Western, the Lancers a rather more picturesque embodiment of the Cavalry. Indeed a number of easterns were remade as westerns simply by indiscriminately switching locations and villains: John Ford's *The Lost Patrol* (1934), with its marauding Arabs repeatedly attacking the dwindling British military unit, was remade as *Bad Lands* (1939) which had the Apache Indians as villains, again as *Sahara* (1943) with the Nazis as villains and again as a Second World War drama, *Baatan* (1943). The ferociously evil oriental, who first appeared on the silver screen with the birth of the cinema, remains consistent, indeed has found a new lease of life exactly at the point where standard westerns became politically problematic: the Arab terrorists of *Exodus* (1960); the deranged Mahdi of *Khartoum* (1966); the evil and dangerous Chinese of *The Face of Fu Manchu* (1965); the sadistic and inhuman Turks of *Midnight Express* (1978); the mad terrorists of *The Ambassador* (1984) and equally mad hostage-takers of 'the fundamentalist state' in *Iron Eagle* (1985); the Chinatown mobsters of the *Year of the Dragon* (1985); the devious Arab villains of *Jewel of the Nile* (1985); the Palestinian terrorists of *Delta Force* (1986); the power-mad leader of the Crimson Jihad in *True Lies* (1994); the Algerian terrorists in *Executive Decision* (1996); the Arab terrorists of *The Siege* (1998).

Hollywood films place the Orient, as Alan Nadel notes, 'at a double remove from the source of its representation. For American audiences, the exotic Other is contained within the equally exotic norms of late nineteenth century England'.[36] The British films of the 1960s and 1970s filtered the East through a colonial lens – the beleaguered British regiment fighting the natives in *Khartoum*, or Kenneth More saving the day against implacable enemies in *North West Frontier*. In the Hollywood product, the British regiment is replaced by the CIA thus 'normalising our understanding of the East through a recognisable Western romance'.[37] In *Khartoum*, the Mahdi of the Sudan is portrayed as a deranged religious fanatic who is happy to slaughter the Egyptians and the Sudanese who don't accept him as the 'Chosen One'. General Gordon, in contrast, is a personification of reason and civility. Not surprisingly, Gordon, the colonizer, is loved by the Sudanese who welcome him to Khartoum. But what motivates the Mahdi? 'I will make Holy War' the Mahdi tells Gordon because 'the Prophet Muhammad, peace and blessings be upon him, has appeared to me in a vision and instructed me to attack Khartoum with fire and sword . . . and terror will inflict and subdue my enemies as far as Mecca, Baghdad and Constantinople'. At the end of the film, the Mahdi's fanatical and marauding Sudanese spear the outnumbered and besieged Gordon.

The Hollywood Arab terrorist films, such as *Delta Force*, *Executive Decision*, *True Lies* and *The Siege*, follow a similar pattern – but, of course, unlike poor Gordon the CIA agents get to 'kick ass' and fly the flag for civilization. In *Delta Force* the terrorists who take over a plane are Palestinians; in *Executive Decision* they are Algerian. Just like *Khartoum*'s Mahdi, they are totally ignorant of

Islam; they do not even know which direction to face when praying
or indeed how to pray – they bow down whenever and wherever it
takes their fancy. This is a persistent piece of significant ignorance,
repeated even where the Muslim character is intended to be
sympathetic. Look at Morgan Freeman's noble Moor in the Kevin
Costner *Robin Hood* (1991). The film opens with stock imagery of
Muslim brutality, Robin Hood is to have a hand chopped off in a
Muslim dungeon replete with the engines of torture. He is saved
from this fate by the 'good' Moor played by Freeman, who then
accompanies Robin Hood back to England. The black Moor is
given a certain dignity and permitted to demonstrate a learning and
philosophy beyond the experience of the Crusaders; so far we have
stereotype mingled with a degree of historic verisimilitude. Why
then, when it comes to prayer, could the makers of the film not find
out how Muslims pray, or indeed what is the content of their
prayers? It is a curious nodule of persistent unwillingness to be
informed. But like all other representations of Muslims at prayer,
Morgan Freeman mouths nonsense and kneels, bends and knocks
his head on the ground in straightforward parody. Fanatical
Muslims incapable of offering their daily prayers have actually
landed, with all their lurking menace, in *True Lies* and *The Siege*:
they are wandering about the US armed to the teeth with all sorts
of nuclear devices. *The Siege* actually depicts a United States as
beleaguered as Gordon in *Khartoum*. The plot of *Executive
Decision* is typical of this genre. Algerian terrorists hijack a plane.
Their leader, as deranged and absurdly fanatic as the Mahdi, issues
a characteristic demand:

This is Al Tar. I have a message for the American president. The
London bombing will have indicated the strength of my resolve. I am
in control of flight 343. This aircraft and its passengers shall remain in
my custody until Abu Jafa, criminally held against his will, is released
from captivity. My instructions are to be followed precisely, no
theatre, no negotiation. El Said Jafa will be released and taken to
Gatwick airport where a private jet will be given clearance to land,
then allowed to leave with him. Upon the release of our leader, flight
343 will continue on to Washington where half the passengers will be
exchanged for fuel and for fifty million in gold bullion. Abu Jafa must
be airborne and in communication with me by 6am Greenwich mean
time or the citizens of London will suffer another punishment on your
behalf that will make today's bombing pale in comparison.

Washington dispatches a special force to sort out the lunatics. Using an extraordinary plane called 'Remora', the special force is secretly spirited on board the hijacked plane. But things go wrong, the military commander leading the team dies. It is left to David Grant, a Pentagon official, to kill the terrorists, with a little help from the airhostess, rescue the hostages and land the plane safely without the on-board bomb going off. Naji, the terrorist leader, is a totally evil man who is motivated by nothing except his own bestial nature. When Jafa is freed and tries to convince Naji to let the hostages go, Naji refuses – he is not evil for nothing! Speaking as though he lived in the Middle Ages, Naji declares:

> I rejoice in your freedom Abu Jafa, Allah has blessed us. A great destiny awaits us both. In a few hours you will see I have achieved a glorious victory on your behalf. All the people of Islam will embrace you as their leader . . . the sword of Allah and with it I will strike deep into the heart of the infidel.

When Naji's second-in-command asks him to abandon the mission, Naji tells him:

> Allah has chosen us for a task, far greater than Jafa's freedom. We are the true soldiers of Islam, our destiny is to deliver the vengeance of Allah into the belly of the Infidel.

For dissension in the ranks Naji shoots his subordinate and proceeds to kill anyone in sight before he is shot himself. People who live and die at the whim of a tyrant are, as we have seen, the essence of Oriental despotism, a foundational part of the stereotype of the Orient.

In some cases, the leading terrorist gets to make a speech to justify his actions. Aziz, the terrorist leader of 'Crimson Jihad' in *True Lies*, is described in the film as 'really hardcore, highly fanat-ical, the man's a real psycho, he's been linked to dozens and dozens of car bombings'. He is motivated solely by revenge, and demon-strates his evil by both possessing nuclear weapons and his willing-ness to use them. Like the Mahdi in Khartoum, he equates truth with power and at the key moment in the film speaks in Arabic: 'in ninety minutes a ball of holy fire will light up the sky to show to the world that we speak the truth'. So what motivates Aziz? In his video-taped demand Aziz declares:

> You have killed our women and our children, bombed our cities from afar like cowards, and you dare to call us terrorists! Now the

oppressed have been given a mighty sword with which to fight back at their enemies. Unless you, America pulls all military forces out of the Persian Gulf area immediately and forever, Crimson Jihad will reign fire on one major US city each week until our demands are met. First we will detonate one weapon on this uninhabited island as a demonstration of our power and Crimson Jihad's willingness to be humanitarian. However, if these demands are not met, Crimson Jihad will reign fire on one major American city each week.

At the end of *Khartoum*, there is a long and sentimental narration, basically justifying colonialism, singing the praises of Gordon and the sacrifices he made for Britain. The Arab terrorist films conclude with a similar homily on the American way of life. At the end of *Delta Force*, for example, after the hostages have been freed and Major McCoy has beaten all terrorists to pulp, cans of Budweiser are served all round to the passengers as they sing the American national anthem in celebration of the work of the CIA.

The Orient of Islam remains consistent on film, it is innately evil for the reason it has always been so in the annals of Orientalism: fanatical attachment to false religion. Other Orients also remain in consonance with their Orientalist history. D.W. Griffith is the inventor of much of the grammar of modern cinema. His *Birth of a Nation* (1915) is an epic about the American Civil War that ends as a peon of praise to the Ku Klux Klan, who emerge to save white womanhood from the evils of miscegenation. The film is as seminal as it is notorious for its racial bigotry. Hollywood has remade American race relations, and after much difficulty got beyond the era of the pickanin, mammie and Step and Fetchit to arrive at the apotheosis of Denzel Washington: the honourable man we can unfailingly rely on to save civilization and uphold the finest American values. In 1919 Griffith made *Broken Blossoms*, another cautionary tale about miscegenation, based on a short story by Thomas Burke rather more explicitly entitled *The Chink and the Child*. Set in London's Limehouse the film concerns Cheng Huan, who has settled in the West intending to be a Buddhist missionary of peace, a touch Jonathon Spence locates in the tradition of Liebniz.[38] What Cheng finds is loneliness and isolation that he staves off with bouts of opium-taking among the taverns and prostitutes of Limehouse. Cheng Huan becomes aware of the plight of his young neighbour, a girl who is violently abused by her drunken father. He offers the girl refuge, and in subtly encoded scenes dresses her in Chinese finery from the curio shop where he works, till she is fit to be a concubine. When the drunken father discovers her whereabouts he breaks in, drags out his daughter whom he proceeds to beat to death, before being shot by Cheng Huan, who then kills himself. Spence seems to feel Griffith is presenting a sympathetic portrayal of the Oriental, though, as he points out in his discussion of the poems of Bret Harte about Chinese labourers in nineteenth-century America, intended sympathy can merely reconfirm the very prejudice they seek to expose. China began as equivocal in Orientalist annals, so in this film with no redeeming characters perhaps this is consistency. Certainly, stock aspects of the constructed stereotype are present in the opium addiction, the imagery of the concubine, and there is lust for white flesh, even if unfulfilled. Bret Harte and Mark Twain, who both wrote many poems, stories and plays about Chinese immigrant workers and the Chinatowns of America, popularized another stock Chinaman, the comic buffoon who speaks only pidgin. One such character they created was Hop Sing. It is worth noting that this is also the name of the comic relief cook who serves the Cartwright family in the long-running television series *Bonanza*. Many of the episodes of this television series were devoted to popularizing revisionism of American race relations in respect of Afro-Americans and Native Americans, but Hop Sing always remained Hop Sing.

The most notable screen presentation of China *qua* China is *The Good Earth*, the 1937 blockbuster, hugely successful at the box office and the Oscars. The film is based on the book of the same name by Pearl S. Buck. Buck was a missionary, born into a missionary family living and working in China, and her most famous book was written in China. Her former husband, another China missionary, assisted Wittfogel by providing him with economic information he had gathered about Chinese agriculture. For all that, *The Good Earth*, as film and book, piles stereotype on stereotype of Orientalist imagery. Its China is timeless, lacking all sense of connection to historic period. Published in 1931 the wars and rumours of wars it contains would have been the dislocations produced by the nationalist uprising of Chiang Kai-shek, but they are unnamed, unspecified and about as elemental as the flood and plague of locusts that also feature as major plot developments. The focus of the story is the lifecycle of the peasant farmer Wang Lung and the former indentured domestic slave he marries, O Lan. Tied to the earth and the struggle to make a living these peasants may be, and thus universalized to some extent, but there is a remoteness about them that is impenetrable. Even more noticeable in the book than the film is the coldness and personal distance, the cold-hearted calculation in human relationships that is innate to the characters, not just a function of the circumstances. The pride at having a first-born son does not translate into fatherly affection, the children are forgotten appendages once born; the heroic wife who bears all the drudgery heaped upon her with unfailing nobility is cast aside for a concubine; Wang Lung is betrayed by his nephew; his sons scheme against him in his old age. There is a bestiality about the grinding poverty in which the married life of Wang Lung and O Lan begins, but the bestiality is carried throughout. The couple endures all the possible vicissitudes China has to offer and by gratuitous fortune rise through all the levels of Chinese society. There are no redeeming features of the portrait of Chinese society, it is all bestial venality, ground into the earth or grasping after more wealth and indulging in all the pleasure of squandering money on opium and concubines once wealth is acquired. The appropriate comparison is to examine *The Good Earth* and John Ford's *The Grapes of Wrath* (1940). There are many comparable elements in the two films but only in *The Grapes of Wrath* can the Joad family achieve true iconic nobility because they are 'Us', fully human and humanized. When Grandma Joad says 'We are the people' she mouths a particular statement that does not and cannot be extended to Wang Lung and O Lan, for all that they tug at our heart strings they are beyond 'our' knowing or being among 'the people' because they are trapped in the perpetual Otherness they represent, the Orient. Hollywood has had a strong relationship with missionary China; it won an Oscar for Gregory Peck as the dedicated catholic priest who made no impact on the Otherness of China in *Keys of the Kingdom* (1944). There were more Oscars for *Inn of the Sixth Happiness* (1958), in which Ingrid Bergman played the missionary Gladys Aylward. In all the films, China is cruel, despotic, wrapped in tradition, chaotic, a corrupt 'ruin on the edge of the world' – as it was for Herder – and perennially resistant to change and the West.

When the Chinese come within Western society, Chinatown is not simply the locale of the comic buffoon, pidgin-speaking laundryman. Chinatown, by convention from Conan Doyle to Sax Rohmer, is a den of iniquity and lurking menace within. It is the abode of that stock embodiment of Chinese cruelty and malign intent, Fu Manchu, whose name spells the Yellow Peril, whose objective is to establish a 'universal Yellow Empire'. The heartless cruelty of Fu Manchu revives the imagery of *Galeote Pereira*, first written in the sixteenth century, which itself depends on the imagery of the Mongol hordes and Marco Polo, the beginning of Western representation of China. As Spence notes, 'with Fu Manchu the depiction of the evil Chinese took an enduring and definitive international form'.[39] In the Hammer Fu Manchu films, it is ancient knowledge that would enable Fu Manchu, 'cruel, callous and the most evil and dangerous man in the world', to subdue the West. In *The Face of Fu Manchu* (1965), the special knowledge that Fu Manchu seeks is described simultaneously as the 'Black Hill Poppy' and 'Secret of Universal Life': it can be used, on the one hand, to destroy the West, and on the other, to attain eternal life for the evil Orient. But Fu Manchu cannot acquire the knowledge himself – even though he is from Tibet, he cannot speak the authentic language; even though the knowledge originates from Tibet, the gate-keeper and protector of this knowledge is a Western expert from the Museum of Oriental Studies. So cinema reiterates the message of Orientalism: the West alone knows, it teaches true authenticity to the East; and the secrets of the East are safe in the hands of the West while the Orient cannot be trusted with them. As we hear a grateful Dalai Lama declare at the end of the film, only with 'the tireless efforts of the foreigner' can the evil of Fu Manchu be contained and lethal knowledge be kept safe. It is worth noting that in virtually all the films mentioned the principal Oriental characters are played by Caucasian actors who give us, appropriately enough, a representation of a representation. Not even Charlie Chan, the inscrutable Oriental detective, was played by a Chinese actor, his most famous screen persona was provided by Walter Oland. He was also played in a number of films by John Carradine, whose son David Carradine has made a career out of recycling Orientalist imagery in the television series *Kung Fu* and *Kung Fu: The Legend Continues*. Chinatown as a place where all the old Chinese evils and perennial viciousness is alive is located within 'the city' and 'the precinct' created for *Kung Fu: The Legend Continues*.

Ancient knowledge and its power are the problem in another recent excursion into the Orient. In *Aladdin* (1992) it is the genie's 'phenomenal cosmic power' that needs to be tamed and brought into the service of America. Aladdin is perhaps the most culturally violent of all Disney animations. At the beginning of the film, our hero is simply Aladdin, the servant of God, but by the end of the story, having realized truth and beauty, he says, 'just call me Al'. The only thing that finally separates Aladdin from a normal Mid-western Caucasian boy is his slight brown colouring. The film is totally steeped in Orientalism. The good guys are all clean-shaven, the bad guys have facial hair typically associated with Easterners and other evil characters. The streets are lined with bartering Arabs and Hindu fakirs and 'Araby' is the land of the exotic. Women are portrayed as erotic, swaying about, wearing the briefest of harem costumes. Even though the genie was trapped in the Arab world, he only knows Western culture, and sings with all the inherent prejudices of Orientalism:

> Oh I come from a land, from a faraway place, where the caravan camels roam;
> Where they cut off your ear if they don't like your face;
> It's barbaric, but hey, its home.

Disney responded to Arab-American complaints by changing the last line for the video release. Hardly a major concession, when the concentrated potency that means barbarism in the line that was not changed, cruel punishment at the whim of a despot, is barbarism that does not need to speak its name to be easily identifiable; that is why stereotypes exist. Like nuclear power, the genie's power can be used for evil purposes as Jafar illustrates when he uses it to become the most powerful sorcerer on Earth. Drunk with his newly acquired power, Jafar transforms into pure dark energy complete with the insignia of nuclear power! Only when the story is secularized, with Allah thrown out and Al thrown in, and Aladdin and Jasmine have been turned into good American citizens, is the knowledge and power of genie liberated for good. Now the genie can

> lead us – as his goofy hat suggests – from the confinement that typifies Eastern culture in the film to its preferable substitution as a form of Western representation. He can convince us that the world is not only safe but also a terrific tourist attraction, exotic in its look but Western in its conventions and values; in short, a great place to visit, even if you wouldn't be allowed to live there.[40]

Within its deploying of familiar Orientalist imagery, *Aladdin* has accomplished the task of contemporary Orientalism – it has ended

history by totally remaking, improving, redeeming and thus effectively abolishing the Orient. *Aladdin* is not only far removed from the
original story, it is also radically different from earlier versions of the
Arabian Nights, from which the Disney production draws most of its
events and images. Before Hollywood discovered a purpose and
meaning for Muslim fanatics it utilized the Orient of the *Arabian
Nights* as a palace of desires and land of wonders, for exotic escapist
entertainment. In the history of film, Orients continue to be remade
according to changes in the agenda of Western interests and fashion.
It has always been a product of diverse images and playing up one
aspect, such as the exotic Orient, does not totally delink it from other
aspects, such as the brutal, barbaric fanatical Orient; it is a matter of
emphasis and choice determined by those with authority over this
tradition, the writers and artists of the West. There are some morals
to be learnt, for example, from the two earlier versions of *The Thief
of Baghdad*. The Raul Walsh film of 1924 suggests that happiness has
to be earned and it attributes this theme to the Qur'an. The Michael
Powell *et al.* version of 1940 argues for political reform. Abu, the
thief of the story, is a street-smart kid who helps the true prince to
reclaim his throne from the evil Jafar. Jafar was able to usurp the
throne because the prince had lost touch with his people. Abu reme-
dies this shortcoming and thus enables the peasants to rise up to a
rebellion in support of the prince. In contrast, the only moral that
Aladdin invokes is total embrace of Pax Americana. When compared with other efforts in the *Arabian Nights* territory, *Aladdin*
appears as positively despicable. The Sindbad films with Ray Harry-
hausen dynamation – *The Seventh Voyage of Sindbad* (1958), *The
Golden Voyage of Sindbad* (1974), *Sindbad and the Eye of the Tiger*
(1977) – retain the flavour of the culture and society where the story
was originally used to convey a moral message. In *The Golden
Voyage of Sindbad*, Sindbad's journey, to find the amulet that would
stop the evil prince Koura from attaining Absolute Power and taking
over the fabulous city of Marabia, is essentially a journey of self-
discovery. The amulet can be used for good or evil and Sindbad's
goal is to ensure that it is used for the purpose of good. When
Sindbad invokes Allah it is to ask for his guidance to be good. For
him belief is a conscious choice. As he tells his sidekick, 'there is an
old proverb, which I choose to believe: Trust in Allah, tie up your
camel'. At the end of his journey, he reconfirms his faith and discovers that freedom is more important than riches. He thus refuses

to wear the 'crown of untold riches' and returns it to its rightful owner with the words: 'did not Allah deliver this into my hands from the fountain of destiny itself to rest upon your head?' While Hollywood invariably portrays Muslims, Chinese and Indians as crooks, warlords and terrorists, the Orient itself is represented as an exotic, seedy place where life is cheap but sensual pleasures are aplenty. From Valentino's *The Sheikh* (1921) onwards, all lands east of the West have been depicted as arenas of sexual licence and perversion where women (and boys) are easy and unspeakable things happen. From the scantily-clad harem women and brutally nasty despots of *Arabian Nights* (1942) to the titillation and camp dances of *Cleopatra* (1934 and 1963) to the Arab prince of *The Harem* (1985), who is into white slavery, to the cheap prostitutes and typhoid-infected primitive Algeria of *The Sheltering Sky* (1990) – the list of films with strong Orientalist messages is considerable and diverse. The Orient is there always as a measure of Otherness, as a permanent witness to the superiority of the Western civilization and an eternal justification for the domination of the West over the non-West. Their laws, their traditions, their customs – the whole damn society needs a strong dose of good, old-fashioned liberal values. *Midnight Express* sums up the entire message. It tells the story of a young American, Billy Hayes, who is caught attempting to smuggle drugs in Istanbul. The Turkish judges decide to make an example of him and Billy is sent to prison for 30 years. Most of the film is about Billy's treatment at the hands of Turkish guards. Now prison guards tend to be sadistic, as we have learned from such films as *Cool Hand Luke* (1967) to the *Shawshank Redemption* (1994), but this lot are true and original barbarians. *Midnight Express* recreates the entire spectrum of the violent, faithless and inhuman Saracens of the Middle Ages. The guards are used as a metaphor for Turkish society itself: they have no civilization worthy of the name, or any sense of society: Billy tells the judge: 'the concept of a society is based on its sense of justice . . . but you wouldn't know'. The entire Turkish judicial system is corrupt, as Billy's English fellow inmate tells him: 'all lawyers here are bent, it's an occupational necessity . . . if you are suspected of honesty, you're disbarred'; Turks are innately treacherous: 'everyone goes round stabbing everyone else in the ass, that's Turkish revenge'; and they are all homosexuals to boot: 'everyone does it every chance they get'. In contrast, Billy and his

English friend Jimmy, both convicted drug smugglers, are innocent, humane and very strong compared to the cowardly Turkish police who are so stupid that they allow Billy to escape by the simple expedient of walking out dressed as a guard. Billy's sentiments, as expressed to the judge, are actually the judgement of the film: 'for a nation of pigs, it sure is funny you don't eat 'em . . . I hate you, your nation and people'. *Midnight Express* was one of the most influential films of the late 1970s – it colours the image and representation of Turkey to this day.

The perception of the East as a place of sensual delight, so deeply ingrained in the Western psyche, is neatly summed up by *Don Juan De Marco* (1995). Johnny, the young hero from Queens, New York, believes that he is Don Juan. He is unhappy, bored and disillusioned with his everyday life and wants to commit suicide. The myths and fantasies that he has built up around him act like a bubble, as an escape from his unhappy reality. The stories he tells Mickler, the psychiatrist, about his imagined life are first-rate Oriental fantasies: he was sold into slavery in Arabia where one of the wives of the ruling Sultan bought him. He stayed in the Sultan's harem dressed as a woman. And so, every day for two years, he made love to the Sultan's wives – 1500 in all! After two years, Don Juan gets tired of all the women and escapes on a ship. The ship is caught in a tropical storm and Don Juan, the sole survivor, is washed up on the desert island of Eros, where he meets the most beautiful woman he has ever seen, Donna Anna. They fall in love at first sight, live on the beach and vow that they will be together forever. But when Anna hears that he has been with 1500 women, she leaves him. He is so heartbroken that he wants to die. At the end of the film, Don Juan, now cured of his fantasies, and Mickler, accompanied by his wife, go off to the Paradise Island of Eros. There, having realized that his own life has lost its fire and become monotonous, Mickler rekindles the long-lost passion for his wife. And to finish the fantasies perfectly, there on the beach is Donna Anna who has been waiting all eternity for Don Juan to return. The East is thus a perfect canvas for the fulfilment and true realization of the West. At the end of the twentieth century, *Don Juan De Marco* reiterates the Orientalist messages relayed at its beginning: it is highly derivative and reminiscent of the previous *fin de siècle* exoticism of Pierre Lotti, whose stories of ennui and sexual liberation in Oriental settings inspired a whole generation of French writers to turn their gaze on the exotic Orient.

The Postmodern
Future

We have seen that Orientalism is very much alive in contemporary cultural practice. All of its main tropes have been seamlessly integrated into modernity. While it is not a monolithic discourse, Orientalism does demonstrate a consistent character throughout history. It has different stylistic moments, diversity of opinions, changing fashions and emphasis. Nevertheless, it has reworked itself from one historic epoch to another, from the Middle Ages to the 'Age of Discovery' to the Enlightenment to colonialism to modernity, maintaining conventional representations of 'the Orient' at the forefront of the European mind. The diversity within Orientalism is similar, for example, to the different styles that we find in Orientalist painting. We can, after the 'Orientalism: Delacroix to Klee' exhibition at the Art Gallery of New South Wales, Australia[1] identify at least eight key stylistic periods in Orientalist painting: Classic Orientalism, The Expanding East, The Ancient East, The Gerome Paradigm, Neo-Romantics, Impressionists and Plein-Artists, Symbolists and Decorators, and Avant-Garde and Colonial Art. The exhibition opens with works by Ingres and Delacroix and shows how the classical and romantic representation of the Orient is constantly reinvested and taken in new directions by succeeding styles. The styles of painting change, but they change within well-established contours. As a general discourse of representation, Orientalism has followed a similar path in history. The distinctive art forms and communication channels of each era recycled standard imagery, iconography and mythology that keeps the past present and Orientalism fully alive and functioning.

Under postmodernism, Orientalism continues its conventional

role of caricaturing and ideologically silencing the civilizations of Asia. We can see this process in action in a host of postmodern com- modities, in particular computer and arcade games, many of which are based on Hollywood films. Computer games, such as *Coloniza- tion*, *Merchant Colony*, *Empire* and *The Settlers*, are postmodern repositories for old conventions of representing the non-West; they simply regurgitate the nineteenth-century European vision of the colonies, repackaged as home entertainment. *Colonization*, for example, invites its players, without even a hint of irony, to con- tinue 'the tradition of civilization' and challenges them to 'colonize' the exotic and stupid natives all over again to 'create a new nation'. *The Settlers* has bored gods who look for amusement by kidnapping representatives of ancient Asian and Egyptian races. These people are then placed on virgin islands where they have to establish settle- ments and defeat each other! Other games such as *Big Red Adven- ture* and *Death Gate* re-run the so-called 'Voyages of discovery'. In *Prince of Persia* (parts 1 and 2), you have standard Oriental women with their skimpy dresses, the stock evil Vizir, Jafar, and an All- American Persian hero, complete with a turban, who has to rescue the persecuted and imprisoned princess. From the most contem- porary source children effortlessly ingest a point of continuity, an extensive tradition, a stance that incorporates a coherent body of ideas.

Continuous repackaging of representation is not just the province of games. It is also present, without critique or critical con- sciousness in 'edutainment' CD-ROMs that combine information with entertainment, and serve as potent educational tools. Despite the supposed capacity of information technology to increase the availability of information, the finite capacity of such 'edutainment' tools makes selection paramount. Thus, Orientalism finds a con- temporary voice both in the process of selection as well as in the actual content. Indeed, such tools do not merely perpetuate Orien- talist representation, they further the process of Orientalism in new ways. CD-ROM encyclopaedias and multimedia packages such as *Microsoft Bookshelf*, *Microsoft Encarta*, the *Compton Interactive Encyclopaedia*, *Hutchinson History Library* and Dorling Kinders- ley's *History of the World* filter history through the lens of America. The most effective market for such products generates a presen- tation of content that subsumes all history and representation as a reflection of itself. Thereby, all cultures of the world, including those of Europe, are seen from the perspective and through the experience of America, which becomes the new apogee of all human civilizations. The old paradigm of linear progress, from the cave to the white man, is repackaged with the minor change that the white man at the top of the evolutionary tree is not the Oxford professorial type but Harvard Business School alumni.

In *Microsoft Bookshelf*, for example, the rest of the world becomes an appendage to American civilization. The Encyclopaedia and Almanac that are part of the package are dominated by their extensive reference to American history, society, literary and cultural products – the rest of human history, culture and civilization is presented as secondary and subsidiary and reduced to thumbnail sketches. Islam is dismissed in a few hundred words; Muhammad gets less than a paragraph, which claims that 'Islam has enshrouded Muhammad's life in a mass of legends and traditions'. The torch of civilization starts in Europe and is passed westwards to America. As we move through time the Almanac dwells more and more effectively on those matters that led inevitably to the establishment of the United States of America; once it is in historical existence it dwells unfailingly on those items which are important within the sensibilities of the United States, occurred within them or to their citizens. Dorling Kindersley's *History of the World* practises a similar variety of Orientalism.[2] From the conclusion of the Second World War, it views the whole world through the America's Cold War perspective. Modern history is thus divided into an ideological battle between American democracy, with its libertarian freedom, and its benighted communist opponent, whose failure is amply detailed. The history of Asia is also subjected to American Orientalism. Japan, for example, makes its appearance through the arrival of the American Captain Perry who forces it to open itself to the world and provides the impetus for the Meiji reform, the overthrowing of the unpopular Shogunate. The essence of the Meiji reform, we are told, is the adoption of Western standards and technology by Japan. The only other mention of Japan in modern times is as America's opponent in the Pacific in the Second World War. The consequence of this battle is the eventual independence of all the countries of Southeast Asia from European rule (the natives, of course, played no part in gaining their own independence!), with a fleeting mention that the Philippines had been ruled by the United States and acquired independence in

1947. In defeat Japan acquires democracy under the tutelage of its conqueror. Asia in the modern world is described through the Vietnam War and Maoist China. In China, we learn that a once popular Maoism became Communist oppression under the Great Leap Forward and Cultural Revolution. But after the death of Mao, Communist leaders in China 'looked for ideas and money from the United States, Japan and others' having decided it was permissible 'for people to buy goods and improve the quality of their life through private enterprise'. The Vietnam War is relevant because 58,000 Americans died there from 1961–73 and spawned an anti-war protest movement in the United States – all the representation of the war centres on the American experience, whose presence is explained solely by the need to oppose Communism. As far as Islam is concerned, its only useful function is to provide cheap oil for the US; so 'oil and Islam' are a combined category that turns all the racist stereotypes of classic Orientalism into the most pernicious of stereotypical contemporary statements. So another era remakes the Orient providing potent and blatant ideology packaged as history and information. Deploying history in episodic compartments enables Orientalism to thrive in its diverse ability to provide whatever explanation is needed at a particular time. The Orient has a history, one that is summed up in the old convention of 'tradition' as unaltering, inflexible imposition and retold as history through the ideological strictures of Western perceptions. In short, Orientalism is revisited in all its patronizing, condescending and racist characteristics.

One of the main features of postmodern times is globalization. The postmodern world is a world of shrinking boundaries, instant communication, and a popular culture that straddles the globe. It is a mass market where Western entertainment consciously creates its products for a global audience, diminishing both the West and the rest. It is also a world dominated by a single superpower; a world where the old European colonialism has been replaced by neo-imperialist superpower politics of a single superpower. In such a world, Orientalism is transformed into an expression of globalized power and becomes both an instrument for exercising that power and containing perceived threats to that power. The iconic symbol of the 'Arab terrorist' as a general representation of Islam, for example, emerged, as I argued in Chapter 4, as a direct product of the threats that America perceived from Islam. It is a representational response to the short-lived rise in oil prices, the event of the Iranian revolution, the general cultural awakening in the Muslim world, and the activities of various surrogate allies that turn into demon opponents. These events straddle the period of the evaporation of the 'Communist bloc'. The vacuum created by the need to embrace the newly redeemed peoples of Russia and Eastern Europe as prodigals returned was readily filled by any increased sensitivity to an older threat to unquestioned American political and cultural domination. Orientalism as scholarship and social process has been complicit in a new round of demonization of Islam and Muslim fundamentalism, effected by refreshing centuries-old stereotypes, and the substitution of Kaleshnikov and Stinger missile for scimitar.

Japan also faces a similar process of Orientalism. Just as Christendom saw Islam as a 'problem' at the beginning of the millennium, America now confronts 'the problem of Japan' at the end of the millennium. In both cases a process of representation contains and manages 'the problem'. Although Japan never became a Western colony, it violently ejected Christian missionaries and rigorously contained European merchants and diplomats. It has conventionally been seen, like the rest of the Orient, as an exotic culture, the land of the geisha. Japan has been admired for its aesthetics (exquisite gardens, curious architecture, strange *kabuki* theatre and funny tea-ceremonies) and feared for its inhuman martial traditions (*samurai, bushido, ninja, kamikaze*). The Japanese themselves were seen as emotionless, robot-like people hermetically sealed in their Zen spirituality and martial aestheticism. However, unlike the rest of the Orient, Japan discovered its own past. Japanese studies remained largely in the hands of Japanese experts and the West could not exercise the kind of authority it took for granted in the case of Islam, India and China. Having defeated Japan and its historic traditions in the apocalyptic climax of the Second World War, all this presented no problem as long as Japan focused on imitating the West, absorbing and regurgitating Western technology, borrowing and reinterpreting Western ideas. It remained tame and contained. Such a Japan provided a vivid demonstration of the linear progress of history towards the apex of the West and reaffirmed Western superiority. It was a Japan that always said 'yes' to Western demands. But, as the title of Shintaro Ishihara's influential book suggests, that Japan is no more: instead we

now have *The Japan That Can Say No*.³ It's a new Japan that cele-
brates Asian values and, occasional economic setbacks notwith-
standing, has confidence in its own future. Moreover, it is a
technologically advanced Japan that has 'Japanized' technology
itself. 'If the future is technological', note David Morley and Kevin
Robins, 'and if technology has become "Japanised"', then the syllo-
gism would suggest that the future is now Japanese too. The postmodern era will be the Pacific era. Japan is the future, and it is a
future that seems to be transcending and displacing Western modernity'.⁴ Suddenly, Japan becomes a 'problem' and a threat. Representations of Japan now take on a decidedly black tone.

We move from the *Teahouse of the August Moon* (1956) phase,
where Marlon Brando played the engaging Japanese peasant who
acts as intermediary and translator for the American victors and
educators of the Reconstruction. The innocent and well-meaning
Americans must tutor the age-old traditions of Japan, which seem
to centre around a geisha house, and mould them into an acceptable modernity. Brando's character is a cunning, artful but ultimately humorous scamp. In films like *Black Rain* (1989), where an
evil Japanese is going to swamp America with counterfeit dollars,
and the overtly racist *Rising Sun* (1993), whose chief villain Eddie
Sakamura, the executive of a Japanese corporation, occupies a
shadowland between business and crime, the Japanese are given
another side of the classic Orientalist treatment. An episode of the
popular television series *LA Law* provides us with an entire discourse on 'the problem' of Japan. It concerns the case of three
American executives whose company was bought by a Japanese
corporation with assurances they would retain their posts, only to
find themselves sidelined and then fired. To win the case the Afro-
American lawyer, encouraged by his Hispanic colleague, knows
what is required: simply play the racist card. The lawyer demon-
strates the inherent difference and inflexibility of Japanese corporate culture, employees must become Japanized, and such a culture
has no place for working women. In his summation the Afro-
American lawyer sways the jury with a naked appeal to fear of
being swamped by a yellow peril that is supremacist and racist, that
is buying up all the choice real estate in Los Angles and threaten-
ing to end civilization as we know it. 'Our' side, the *LA Law* lawyer,
wins, securing enormous damages for his clients.

The threat of the Japanese – a robot-like dedication to world

hegemony and swamping of American culture – is personified by
Shredder, the villain of the animation show, *Teenage Mutant Ninja
Turtles*. He lives in a sewer and, unless stopped by the pizza-loving
all-American turtles, will use the Ninja techniques of fighting and
moving like a shadow to erode and undermine American civilization. Such representations are based on the 'fear that Japan's irreducible difference will remain aloof from, and impenetrable to,
Western reason and universalism. A fear, too, that Western culture
might itself be overwhelmed by the Oriental Other'.[5] The combination of this fear and the 'Japan problem' has lead to a new variety
of Orientalism: techno-orientalism, which, in the words of Toshiya
Ueno, 'constructs and presents a Japan as an "automaton culture"
and sees the Japanese as the "automated Other" of the West'.[6] The
reinvented Japan of techno-orientalism – a land of Manga comic
strips and film animations, *Godzilla*, violent films like *Tetsuo*
(1989), video-games, video-cameras, video-phones, techno porn,
faxes, televisions, computers, smart buildings, saturated bullet
trains and overcrowded cities – can be sampled in cyberpunk novels
like William Gibson's *Neuromancer* and futuristic movies like
Blade Runner (1982). 'But there is another', write Morley and
Robins:

> more resentful and more aggressively racist, side to this techno-orien-
> talism. The association of technology and Japaneseness now serve to
> reinforce the image of a culture that is cold, impersonal and machine-
> like, an authoritarian culture lacking emotional connection to the rest
> of the world. The otaku generation – kids 'lost to everyday life' by
> their immersion in computer reality – provide a good symbol of this
> ... These kids are imagined as people mutating into machines; they
> represent a kind of cybernetic mode of being for the future. This cre-
> ates the image of the Japanese as inhuman. Within the political and
> cultural unconscious of the West, Japan has come to exist as the figure
> of empty and dehumanised technological power. It represents the
> alienated and dystopian image of capitalist progress. This provokes
> both resentment and envy. The Japanese are unfeeling aliens; they are
> cyborgs and replicants. But there is also the sense that these mutants
> are now better adapted to survive in the future. The otaku are post-
> modern people. To use Baudrillard's phrase, the future seems to have
> shifted towards artificial satellites.[7]

The images of this inhuman, authoritarian Orient of Japan – a logical extension of Pearl S. Buck's vision of the Chinese – provides us

with yet another connection that goes back through time, through sequences of cold-hearted, remorselessly cruel and evil Oriental villains bent on world domination, all the way to Marco Polo. However, there has never been a need for logic within the patterns, the internal constellation of ideas about any particular Orient; such Orients have never fitted together into a single, consistent monolithic edifice. The Orient is passionless and fanatic; disciplined in the arts of cruelty and licentious and effete; built on family and filial duty and lacking emotional warmth in intimate human relations. A place of bizarre traditions and behaviour that can be comic or menacing and frightening. Only a construct made for present utility in argument can be so many things to so many people at one and the same time. The Orientalist framework is retentive and extensive, old and familiar and refreshed and pressed into new shapes according to present circumstance. Constant accumulation occurs through episodic spurts, the periodic remaking in current circumstances of a particular Orient that somehow never unmakes those ideas that were part of the past. Coherence exists because of the interrelationship of the stereotypes that are deployed to effect a transformation, and the lack of specificity of all Orients, enabling ideas predominant in one Orient to be borrowed and pressed into service in another. In the wonders of the East that are by definition strange and marvellous, everything is possible. So new formulations of Orients emerge from the repository of shared Orientalist understanding, that is assimilated by cultural osmosis from many disparate strands and locations. Different, potentially contradictory ideas about any one Orient inspire not argument, a critical attitude and deconstruction, but constructive mutual reinforcement. The old ideas are retained while new nuances are added and the repertoire goes on expanding. The process is so internalized, so integral to how 'We' think and reason, so unconsciously part of the consciousness of the West, that it can generate a new meaning for the term West, generate a new Orient almost without anyone noticing. In postmodern times, 'the Orient' has been globalized: it is located everywhere and everywhere it can be subjected to Orientalization, from the one ruling perspective that defines itself as West.

So we can now witness the formulation of a new Orient. Europe itself is being transformed into a new Orient *vis-à-vis* America. The American representation of Europe, we can detect, is following the classical patterns of Orientalism. For example, in American films

and television series, the English are being Orientalized. Just as
Orientalism presented the non-European Other as bound and con-
strained by tradition and history, motivated largely by the antique,
so London is presented in American films as though it was frozen
in history. In the London of *Parent Trap* (1998), everyone is rich
and upper-class and the city itself is distinctively archaic, traditional
and 'exotic'. In the popular television situation comedy, *Frasier*,
Daphne speaks with an accent that is supposed to emphasize the
decidedly old and has-been world of the English. In contrast to the
clever and witty Frasier, and his equally urbane brother, Niles,
Daphne is not only stupid but also quite unworldly, reflecting the
antiquated culture of her origin. The English villains of *Die Hard*
(1988) and *Die Hard With A Vengeance* (1995) incorporate all the
characteristics of the 'Arab terrorists': motivated by greed and
revenge, they are inherently evil and violent with not an iota of
humanity. In the two episodes of the popular television show
Friends set in London, the city is depicted solely through stock
stereotypical images – Westminster Abbey, Big Ben, Tower of
London – to emphasize an England trapped in a time warp. In this
episode, one of the leading characters, Ross, is marrying his newly
acquired English girlfriend, Emily. Compared to the three leading
women of the show – Rachel, Monica, Phoebe – who are brainless
but charming, Emily is decidedly charmless, a twit without any wit
who speaks with a funny accent reminiscent of *Frasier*'s Daphne.
Her awful and crooked parents want to use the wedding to squeeze
as much money out of Ross's parents as possible; Ross's father
describes Emily's father as a 'thieving', 'cheap little man'. Emily's
housekeeper comes straight from the nineteenth century: she tells
Phoebe, 'young lady, that is not how one addresses a person on the
telephone. First one identifies oneself, and then politely asks for the
party with whom one wishes to speak.' The ancient church where
Emily wants to have her wedding has been demolished. In a final
coup de grace, Ross has the semi-demolished church restored for
the wedding. The message is clear: England is an antiquated, quaint
little place, inhabited by awful people with peculiar accents, that
needs a dose of superior Americana to rescue it from its own folly.
The British newspapers found this representation of England
'humiliating' and 'insulting': welcome to the Orientalized England.
A very similar scenario, with similar representations, is the sub-
stance of *Three Men and A Little Lady* (1990). The lady of the title

could not be left to the awful fate of being raised in an aristocratic British country mansion by her three all-American 'fathers'. Such representations of the English, containing all the negative attributes of Orientalism, help define the mobility, freedom and innate superiority of the culture of dominance – American culture. Just as Orientalism in the past included the appropriation of all storytelling within the culture of dominance, so now characteristic English stories must be adapted, as must all of history and all other Orients, to fit within or be witnessed by representatives of the culture of dominance, whatever damage this does to literary integrity or common logic. It is not just a case of making such tales suitable for the isolationist reflex of American culture. Orientalism says much more, as we have seen through its history. Orientalism is surrogate self-definition of the dominant culture as much as deployment of the difference of an Orient. True, history will not stay written. It has to be rewritten from the viewpoint of every age – with all the necessary references to its own social conditions, its thoughts and beliefs and its acquisitions. In this way, it becomes comprehensible to the people who live in it. But Orientalism implies something much more, for it is a rewriting through a disproportionate process of relationship in which one part, the Oriental, remains trapped, separate, unheard, though described to enable the freedom of the describing and defining party. In the process of Orientalism and the relationship it structures the describing and described become less intelligible, as they become more familiar, less able to communicate because of the edifice the process constructs, the Orient.

Postmodernism embraces Orientalism because it is made up of so many of the favoured techniques that define postmodernism. If postmodernism recognizes no reality but only the pleasure principle, what better vehicle could there be than a process that has always constructed Orients as pleasure palaces for the indulgence and self-expression of the 'I', the dominant 'self'? Orientalism has been a vehicle for imaginative appropriation; postmodernism encourages us all to make up our own identity by appropriating eclectically from all of human history and cultures. As description, Orientalism has always indulged in parody, ridicule and pastiche whether to belittle or create frightening demons, whether in lighter or darker mood. The amorphousness of Orientalism, its ability to accumulate and ignore inconsistency exactly fits this temper of postmodernism. Ultimately, Orientalism is a system of representations, a natural expression for postmodernists who argue representation is all we have. So postmodernism tacitly accepts Orientalism, it conforms to its own definition as the inevitable expression of all that is possible. Orientalism, as a definite process in the past, can be the subject of deconstruction; it can receive a postmodern kick as a function of the old metanarratives that are now superseded. But, what is deconstructed is a truncated version of a cultural propensity that still leaves the project of Orientalism in the present, in place, in operation. All the conventions that I have pointed to as Orientalism in this book are postmodern in their characteristics. There is now total self-identity and no escape. We thus return to *M. Butterfly* where the West would rather choose death than give up the pleasure palace of the Orient on aesthetic grounds, for postmodernism is essentially an aesthetic. Postmodernism is thus set to expand the project of Orientalism to new territories and new Orients.

The connective tissue of Orientalism is not its conscious monolithic inflexibility. Orientalism is built out of the constructive imagination of the culture of the West. It is as diverse as the dexterity of Western culture; this is why and how Orientalism as a process has survived, keeping step with the place of its origin and use, a work of change and continuity. Orientalism is memory, imagination and present utility in a process of representation that structures knowledge and information. As such, Orientalism cannot be appreciated only as academic discourse; it is a cultural discourse in the widest possible sense, it is simply what is known and taken for granted. At the level of popular culture, Orientalism is most ubiquitous and most potent. Therefore all conspiracy theories, all attempts to make causal links between government, empire and espionage fail to convince. Direct causation, conscious planning, overt agendas are not the manner in which Orientalism works its effects. Orientalism is more endemic, innate and diverse, it has been around for so long that it is the predisposition that forms the sense of reality itself for the West. And, it is the embedded persistence of a process of unconscious acceptance that makes Orientalism an impasse. The peoples of the various Orients cannot engage in discussion, cannot make themselves heard as they understand themselves, through the background noise that conditions the reception and sensitivities of the peoples of the West. If Orientalism were a conscious work of straightforward causality in knowledge and power it would be much easier to confront and eject. Only by grasping the unconscious, innate and ubiquitous diversity of Orientalism within the self-perception of the West can one make a case for remedy. The remedy must be a new conscious openness to what the peoples of the Orients, the masses to the East of the West, think, know and feel about themselves, their culture and their history. The convention of authenticity needs to be seen as the artifice it is. Change and continuity, distortion and prejudice, reinvention and reformulation, must be accepted as part and parcel of the cultural acumen of all peoples. In which case there is a great deal to discuss between different peoples, East and West, none of whom are standing still. To arrive at a sustainable plural future there must be a process beyond Orientalism. There needs to be a terminus, an end to a process that keeps some people caught in a nexus of untenable recycled ideas. That terminus cannot be acceptance of the classical representations of the Orient, no matter how venerable they have become in the unconscious of the West. Unless the limitations of representation masquerading as reality are perceived and understood, a plural future founded on mutual respect and enhanced mutual understanding is impossible. We will continue to live out the consequences of conflict, mistrust, denigration and marginalization that are the all too real legacy of Orientalism.

Notes

Chapter 1

1 Federici, S., 'The God that never failed: the origins and crises of western civilization' in Silvia Federici (ed.), *Enduring Western Civilisation* (Westport, Connecticut: Praeger, 1995), p. 66.
2 Evidence to Select Committee of the House of Commons (1781) vol. 37, p. 107.

Chapter 2

1 Wright, T. (ed.), *The Travels of Marco Polo* (New York: ASM Press, 1968).
2 Wittfogel, K., *Oriental Despotism* (New York: Vintage Books, 1981).
3 See Wood, F., *Did Marco Polo Go To China?* (London: Secker and Warburg, 1995).
4 See Williams, G.A., *Excalibur* (London: BBC, 1994).
5 Crone, P. and Cook, M., *Hagarism: The Making of the Islamic World* (Cambridge: Cambridge University Press, 1977).
6 Southern, R.W., *Western Views of Islam in the Middle Ages* (Cambridge, Massachusetts: Harvard, 1962), p. 7.
7 Ibid., pp. 23–4.
8 Ibid., p. 25.
9 Gwyn op cit., p. 120.
10 Bacon quoted in Southern, op cit., p. 59.
11 Campbell, M.B., *The Witness and the Other: Exotic European Travel Writing 400–1600* (Ithaca, NY: Cornell University Press, 1988), p. 48.
12 Mandeville, Sir John, *The Travels of Sir John Mandeville* (Harmondsworth: Penguin, 1983), p. 180.
13 Preface to *Travels of Sir John Chardin into Persia and the East Indies* (1686).

14 Quoted by Latham, J.D., 'Arabic and Islamic Studies in the UK', *New Books Quarterly*, 1: 2–3, 1981, pp. 37–8.
15 Hamilton, A., *William Bedwell, the Arabist* (Leiden: Brill, 1985), p. 67.
16 Prideaux, H., *Mahomet: The True Nature of the Imposter Fully Displayed in the Life of Mahomet* (1697).
17 Ibid.
18 Ibid.
19 Heylyn, P., *Cosmographie* (1682).
20 De Baer, E.S. (ed.), *Correspondence of John Locke* (Oxford: Oxford University Press, 1976–), vol. I, p. 353.
21 Maundrell, H., *Journey from Aleppo to Jerusalem at Easter* (1697), p. 53.
22 de Thevenot, A., *Travels of Monsieur de Thevenot into the Levant* (1686), pt i, p. 58.
23 Rycaut, Sir Paul, *Present State of the Ottoman Empire* (1668), p. 32.
24 *Works of Sir William Temple* (1814), vol. III, p. 390.
25 Berniev, F., *Travels in the Mughal Empire* (1914), p. 231.
26 de Thevenot, op cit., pt i, p. 58.
27 Baines, Sir Thomas, *Early Travels Voyages and Travels in the Levant* (1893), p. 271.
28 Terry, E., *A Voyage to the East Indies* (1655), p. 346.
29 Boxer, C. (ed.), *South China in the Sixteenth Century: Being the Narratives of Galeote Pereira, Fr. Gaspar da Cruz, OP, Fr. Martin de Rada, OESA* (London: The Hakluyt Society, second series, 1953).
30 Ricci, M., *China in the Sixteenth Century Journals 1583–1610*, transl. and ed. L. Gallagher (New York: 1953), p. 30.
31 Lach, D. (ed.), *Liebniz Novissima Sinica – Latest News from China* (Honolulu, 1957), pp. 46–7.
32 Montesquieu, *Spirit of the Laws* (1748), p. 280.
33 Voltaire, *History of Manners and Spirit of Nations* (1756), XXIV, pp. 28–9.
34 Ferguson, A., *An Essay on the History of Civil Society*, ed. by D. Forbes (Edinburgh: Edinburgh University Press, 1986).
35 Marshall, P.G. and Williams, G., *The Great Map of Mankind* (London: Dent, 1982), p. 87.
36 von Herder, J.G., *The Outline of a Philosophy of the History of Man* (1784), pp. 197–8, 296.
37 Marshall and Williams, op cit., p. 176.
38 Holwell, J.Z., *Interesting Historical Events relative to the Province of Bengal and the Empire of Indostan* (1767), p. 70.
39 Reynal, A., *A Philosophical and Political History of the Settlement and Trade of the Europeans in the East and West Indies* (1777), vol. 1, p. 38.
40 Marshall, P.G., *The British Discovery of Hinduism in the Eighteenth Century* (Cambridge: Cambridge University Press, 1970), pp. 43–4.

41 Quoted in Marshall, P.G. (ed.), *Writing and Speeches of Edmund Burke* (Oxford: Oxford University Press, 1981), pp. 140–2.
42 Marshall and Williams, op cit., p. 158.
43 Ibid., p. 94.
44 Mandeville, Sir John, *Travels*, op cit., p. 189.
45 Grant, C., letter to Methodist minister Thomas Coke, in *Life of Thomas Coke* (London, 1815), p. 201.
46 Quoted in Kabbani, R., *Europe's Myths of the Orient* (London: Macmillan, 1986), p. 34.
47 Ibid., p. 59.
48 Djait, H., *Europe and Islam* (Berkeley: University of California Press, 1985), p. 29.
49 Doughty, C.M. (1888), *Travels in Arabia Deserta* (New York: Dover, 1979 edn), vol. 1, p. 21.
50 Ibid., vol. 2, p. 405.
51 Ibid., vol. 2, p. 22.
52 Al-Sayyid, A.L., *Egypt and Cromer* (London: John Murray, 1968), p. 77.
53 Ibid., p. 143.
54 Cromer quoted in Said, E., *Orientalism* (London: Routledge and Kegan Paul, 1978), p. 38.
55 Byron, Lord, 'Notes to Childe Harold's Pilgrimage', *The Poetical Works* (London: 1960), p. 884
56 Kabbani, op cit., pp. 84–5.
57 Quoted by Thornton, L., *The Orientalists: Painter-Travellers* (Paris: ARC Edition, 1994), p. 152.
58 Hegel, *Lectures on the Philosophy of History*, quoted by Djait, H., *Europe and Islam* (Berkeley: University of California Press, 1985), p. 80.
59 Said, op cit., p. 154.
60 Spengler, O., *The Decline of the West* (New York: Knopf, 1939).
61 Iqbal, Sir Muhammad, *Reconstruction of the Religious Thought in Islam* (Lahore: Ashraf, 1971), pp. 142–3.
62 Toynbee, A., *A Study of History* (Oxford and London: Oxford University Press and Thames and Hudson, 1972).

Chapter 3

1 Jameelah, M., *Islam and Orientalism* (Lahore: Yusuf Khan, 1971), p. 105.
2 Tibawi, A.L., *English-speaking Orientalists: A Critique of Their Approach to Islam and Arab Nationalism* (London: Luzac, 1964), p. 8.
3 Ibid., p. 9.

4 Ibid., all quotes in paragraph are from p. 11.
5 Ibid., p. 13.
6 Originally published in *Diogène* (1963), 44, pp. 109–42. All quotes taken from Anouar Abdel-Malek, *Civilisation and Social Theory* (London: Macmillan, 1981), where the paper has been reproduced; pp. 75–6.
7 Ibid., p. 76.
8 Ibid., p. 76.
9 Ibid., p. 77.
10 Ibid., p. 77.
11 Ibid., p. 79.
12 Ibid., p. 80.
13 Swettenham quoted in Alatas, S.H., *The Myth of the Lazy Native* (London: Frank Cass, 1977), p. 45.
14 Ibid., p. 72.
15 Ibid., pp. 72–3.
16 Alatas, S.H.,*The Myth of the Lazy Native* (London: Frank Cass, 1977), p. 75.
17 Djait, H., *Europe and Islam* (Berkeley: University of California Press, 1985), pp. 169–70.
18 Ibid., p. 173.
19 Ibid., p. 6.
20 Ibid., all quotes in the paragraph are from pp. 171–2.
21 Ahmad, A., *In Theory: Classes, Nations, Literatures* (London: Verso, 1992), ch. 5.
22 Posthumously collected together in Hodgson, M.G., *Rethinking World History* (Cambridge: Cambridge University Press, 1993).
23 Hodgson, M.G., *The Venture of Islam* (Chicago: University of Chicago Press, 1974; 3 vols).
24 Clifford, J., *The Predicament of Culture: Twentieth-century Ethnography, Literature and Art* (Cambridge, Mass: Harvard University Press, 1988), p. 267.
25 Said, E., *Orientalism* (London: Routledge and Kegan Paul, 1978), p. 1.
26 Ibid., p. 3.
27 Ibid., pp. 41–2.
28 Ibid., p. 203.
29 Ibid., p. 94.
30 Lewis, B., *Islam and the West* (New York: Oxford University Press, 1993).
31 Gellner, E., 'The mightier pen? Edward Said and the double standards of inside-out colonialism', *Times Literary Supplement*, 19 February 1993.
32 Fox, R.G., 'East of Said' in M. Sprinker (ed.), *Edward Said: A Critical Reader* (Oxford: Blackwell, 1992), p. 145.
33 MacKenzie, J., *Orientalism: History, Theory and the Arts* (Manchester: Manchester University Press, 1995), pp. 208–10.

34 Ibid., p. 215.
35 Young, R., *White Mythologies: Writing History and the West* (London: Routledge, 1990), p. 129.
36 Porter, D., 'Orientalism and its Problems' in P. Williams and L. Chrisman (eds), *Colonial Discourse and Post-Colonial Theory* (Hertfordshire: Harvester Wheatsheaf, 1993), p. 151.
37 Ibid., p. 152.
38 Ibid., p. 153.
39 Said, op cit., p. 328.
40 Young, op cit., pp. 227–8.
41 Ahmad, op cit., p. 164.
42 Ibid., p. 168.
43 Young, op cit., p. 127.
44 Richardson, M., 'Enough Said – Reflections of Orientalism', *Anthropology Today*, 6: 4, 1990, pp. 16–19.
45 Said, E., *The Politics of Dispossession* (New York: Pantheon Books, 1994), p. 388.
46 Said, E., *Covering Islam* (New York: Pantheon Books, 1981), p. 41.
47 Said, E., 'Orientalism Reconsidered' in F. Barker *et al.* (eds), *Europe and Its Others* (Colchester: University of Essex, 1985; 2 vols).
48 Said, E., *The World, the Text and the Critic* (Harvard: Harvard University Press, 1983), p. 290.
49 Makdisi, G., *The Rise of Humanism in Classical Islam and the Christian West* (Edinburgh: Edinburgh University Press, 1990); and Makdisi, G., *The Rise of Colleges: Institutions of Learning in Islam and the West* (Edinburgh: Edinburgh University Press, 1981).
50 Said, E., *Representation of the Intellectual* (London: Vintage, 1994).
51 Robbins, B., 'East is a Career' in M. Sprinker (ed.), op cit., p. 50.

Chapter 4

1 This is a contested terrain. See M. Harris's incomprehension in *The Rise of Anthropological Theory* (London: Routledge, 1969), arguing with this point as made by M. Hodgen in *Early Anthropology in the Sixteenth and Seventeenth Centuries* (Philadelphia: University of Philadelphia Press, 1964).
2 Marshall, P.G. and Williams, G., *The Great Map of Mankind* (London: Dent, 1982), p. 143.
3 Cantwell Smith, W., *Islam in the Modern World* (Princeton: Princeton University Press, 1957).
4 Gibb, H.A.R., *Modern Trends in Islam* (Chicago: University of Chicago Press, 1947).
5 Hitti, P.K., *Islam and the West* (Princeton: Von Nostrand, 1962).
6 Cantwell Smith, op cit., p. 110.

7 Cragg, K., as summarized by J. Qureshi in A. Hussain and J. Qureshi *et al.* (eds), *Orientalism, Islam and Islamists* (Battleboro: Amana Books, 1984), pp. 211–13.

8 Anderson, N., *Islam in the Modern World: A Christian Perspective* (Leicester: Apollos, 1990).

9 Crone, P. and Cook, M., *Hagarism: the Making of the Islamic World* (Cambridge: Cambridge University Press, 1977).

10 Cook, M., *Muhammad* (Oxford: Oxford University Press, 1983).

11 Pipes, D., *In the Path of God: Islam and Political Power* (New York: Basic Books, 1954).

12 Binder, L. *Islamic Liberalism* (Chicago: University of Chicago Press, 1988), p. 106.

13 Ibid., p. 107.

14 Cook, op cit., pp. 37, 38.

15 Laffin, J., *The Dagger of Islam* (London: Pan Books, 1991).

16 Fukayama, F., *End of History and the Last Man* (London: Hamish Hamilton, 1992).

17 Huntingdon, S., 'The Clash of Civilizations', *Foreign Affairs*, 72 (3), July/August 1993, pp. 22–49.

18 Soguk, N., 'Reflections on the "Orientalised Orientals"', *Alternatives*, 18, 1993, p. 363.

19 Quoted in Edwards, M., *Raj* (London: Pan Books, 1969), p. 151.

20 Vittachi, V.T., *The Brown Sahib Revisited* (Delhi: Penguin, 1987), p. 14.

21 Singer, M.R., *The Emerging Elite* (Cambridge, Massachusetts: MIT Press, 1964), p. 47.

22 See Ibrahim, S.E. and Hopkins, N.S. (eds), *Arab Society* (Cairo: American University of Cairo Press, 1985).

23 Naipaul, V.S., *Among the Believers: An Islamic Journey* (London: Penguin, 1981).

24 Rushdie, S., *The Satanic Verses* (London: Viking, 1988).

25 Naipaul, op cit., p. 16.

26 Ibid., p. 14.

27 See Geoffrey Chaucer, *The Canterbury Tales: A Selection*, ed. D.R. Howard (New York: Signet Classics, 1969), p. 78.

28 Naipaul, V.S., *Beyond Belief: Islamic Excursions Among the Converted Peoples* (London: Little, Brown, 1998).

29 Daniel, N., *Islam and the West* (Oxford: One World, 1993), p. 17.

30 Nandy, A., *Traditions, Tyranny and Utopias* (New Delhi: Oxford University Press, 1987), p. 15.

31 Updike, J., *The Coup* (New York: Random House, 1978).

32 Caputo, P., *The Horn of Africa* (London: Futura, 1982).

33 Randall, J., *The Jihad Ultimatum* (New York: Pinnacle Books, 1988).

34 Forsyth, F., *The Fist of God* (London: Corgi Books, 1994).

35 Carson, M., *Friends and Infidels* (Black Swan: London, 1989).

36 Nadel, A., 'A whole new (Disney) world order: *Aladdin*, atomic power and the Muslim Middle East' in M. Bernstein and G. Studlar (eds), *Visions of the Orient: Orientalism in Film* (London: I.B. Tauris, 1997), p. 184.
37 Nadel, op cit., p. 185.
38 Spence, J., *The Great Chan's Great Continent: China in Western Minds* (New York: W.W. Norton, 1998), p. 167.
39 Ibid., p. 140
40 Nadel, op cit., p. 199.

Chapter 5

1 For a brief discussion of the exhibition see Beaulieu, J., 'Re-viewing Orientalism', *Third Text*, 43: 98–101, 1998.
2 For a detailed discussion of Dorling Kindersley's *History of the World* see Sardar, Z., *Postmodernism and the Other* (London: Pluto Press, 1998), ch. 3.
3 Ishihara, S., *The Japan That Can Say No* (New York: Simon and Schuster, 1991).
4 Morley, D. and Robins, K., *Spaces of Identity* (London: Routledge, 1995), p. 168.
5 Ibid., p. 162.
6 Ueno, T. (1997) 'Japanimation and Techno-Orientalism' in M.B. Roetto (ed.), *ISEA 96 Proceedings: Seventh International Symposium on Electronic Art* (Rotterdam: ISEA 96 Foundation, 1997).
7 Morley and Robins, op cit., p. 170.

Select Bibliography

Abdel-Malek, A. (1981) *Civilisations and Social Theory*. London: Macmillan.

Ahmad, A. (1992) *In Theory: Classes, Nations, Literatures*. London: Verso.

Ahmed, L. (1992) *Women and Gender in Islam: Historical Roots of a Modern Debate*. New Haven: Yale University Press.

Alatas, S.H. (1977) *The Myth of the Lazy Native*. London: Frank Cass.

Alloula, M. (1986) *The Colonial Harem*, trans. M. Godzich and W. Godzich. Minneapolis: University of Minnesota Press.

Asad, T. (1973) *Anthropology and the Colonial Encounter*. London: Ithaca Press.

Asad, T. (1993) *Genealogies of Religion: Discipline and Reasons of Power in Christianity and Islam*. Baltimore: The Johns Hopkins University Press.

Beaulieu, J. (1998) 'Re-viewing Orientalism', *Third Text*, 43: 98–101.

Bernstein, M. and Studlar, G. (1997) *Visions of the East: Orientalism in Film*. London: I.B. Tauris.

Binder, L. (1988) *Islamic Liberalism*. Chicago: University of Chicago Press.

Brenan, T. (1989) *Salman Rushdie and the Third World*. London: Macmillan.

Campbell, M.B. (1988) *The Witness and the Other: Exotic European Travel Writing 400–1600*. Ithaca: Cornell University Press.

Chow, R. (1993) *Writing Diaspora: Tactics of Intervention in Contemporary Cultural Studies*. Bloomington: Indiana University Press.

Clifford, J. (1988) *The Predicament of Culture: Twentieth-century Ethnography, Literature and Art*. Cambridge, Mass: Harvard University Press.

Clifford, J. (1988) 'On Orientalism', in *The Predicament of Culture: Twentieth-century Ethnography, Literature, and Art*. Cambridge, Mass.: Harvard University Press.

Coury, R. (1997) 'The persistence and rehabilitation of Orientalism', *Third Text*, 39: 67–76.

Daniel, N. (1966) *Islam, Europe and Empire*. Edinburgh: Edinburgh University Press.

Daniel, N. (1979) *Arabs and Medieval Europe*. London: Longman.

Daniel, N. (1984) *Heroes and Saracens*. Edinburgh: Edinburgh University Press.

Daniel, N. (1993) *Islam and the West*. Oxford: One World (original edn, 1960).

Davies, M.W. (1988) *Knowing One Another: Shaping an Islamic Anthropology*. London: Mansell.

Djait, H. (1985) *Europe and Islam*. Berkeley: University of California Press.

Edwards, M. (1969) *Raj*. London: Pan Books.

Fabian, J. (1983) *Time and the Other: How Anthropology Makes Its Object*. New York: Colombia University Press.

Federici, S. (ed.) (1995) *Enduring Western Civilisation*. Westport, Connecticut: Praeger.

Gillespie, M. (1995) *Television, Ethnicity and Cultural Change*. London: Routledge.

Goonatilake, S. (1982) *Crippled Minds: An Exploration into Colonial Culture*. Delhi: Vikas.

Gunny, A. (1996) *Images of Islam in Eighteenth-century Writings*. London: Grey Seal.

Habib, I. (1995) *Essays in Indian History*. New Delhi: Tulika.

Halliday, F. (1993) 'Orientalism and its critics', *British Journal of Middle Eastern Studies*, 20 (2).

Harris, M. (1969) *The Rise of Anthropological Theory*. London: Routledge.

Hodgen, M. (1964) *Early Anthropology in the Sixteenth and Seventeenth Centuries*. Philadelphia: University of Philadelphia Press.

Hodgson, M.G. (1961–74) *The Venture of Islam*. Chicago: University of Chicago Press (3 vols).

Hussain, A. and Querishi, J. *et al*. (eds) (1984) *Orientalism, Islam and Islamists*. Battleboro: Amana Books.

Ishihara, S. (1991) *The Japan That Can Say No*. New York: Simon and Schuster.

Jameelah, M. (1971) *Islam and Orientalism*. Lahore: M.Y. Khan.

Jullian, P. (1977) *Les Orientalistes*. Paris: L'Office du Livre.

Kabbani, R. (1986) *Europe's Myths of the Orient*. London: Macmillan,

Kuper, A. (1988) *The Invention of Primitive Society*. London: Routledge.

Lambropoulos, V. (1993) *The Rise of Eurocentrism: Anatomy of Interpretation*. Princeton: Princeton University Press.

Laroui, A. (1976) *The Crisis of the Arab Intellectual*. Berkeley: University of California Press.

Lawrence, B. (1998) *Shattering the Myth: Islam beyond Violence*. Princeton: Princeton University Press.

Lewis, R. (1996) *Gendering Orientalism: Race, Femininity and Represen-*
tation. London: Routledge.

Lowe, L. (1991) *Critical Terrains: French and British Orientalisms*. Ithaca:
Cornell University Press.

Maalouf, A. (1984) *The Crusades Through Arab Eyes*. London: Al Saqi.

MacKenzie, J.M. (1995) *Orientalism: History, Theory and the Arts*. Manchester: Manchester University Press.

Makdisi, G. (1981) *The Rise of Colleges: Institutions of Learning in Islam*
and the West. Edinburgh: Edinburgh University Press.

Makdisi, G. (1990) *The Rise of Humanism in Classical Islam and the Chris-*
tian West. Edinburgh: Edinburgh University Press.

Mani, L. and Frankenberg, R. (1995) 'The Challenge of Orientalism',
Economy and Society, 14 (2): 174–92.

Marchetti, G. (1993) *Romance and the 'Yellow Peril'*. Berkeley: University
of California Press.

Marshall, P.G. (1970) *The British Discovery of Hinduism in the Eighteenth*
Century. Cambridge: Cambridge University Press.

Marshall, P.G. and Williams, G. (1982) *The Great Map of Mankind*.
London: Dent.

Menon, N. (1993) 'Orientalism and After', *Public Culture*, 6 (1): 65–76.

Michalak, L. (undated) *Cruel and Unusual: Negative Images of Arabs in*
American Popular Culture. Washington, DC: American Arab Anti-
Discrimination Committee.

Mitchell, T. (1988) *Colonizing Egypt*. Cambridge: Cambridge University
Press.

Morley, D. and Robins, K. (1995) *Spaces of Identity: Global Media, Elec-*
tronic Landscapes and Cultural Boundaries. London: Routledge.

Nandy, A. (1983) *The Intimate Enemy*. Delhi: Oxford University Press.

Nandy, A. (1987) *Traditions, Tyranny and Utopias*. New Delhi: Oxford
University Press.

Nielson, J. and Khasawnih, S.A. (1998) *Arabs and the West: Mutual Images*.
Amman: Jordan University Press.

Nochlin, L. (1983) 'The Imaginary Orient', *Art in America*, 71 (5): 118–31,
186–91.

Panikkar, K.M. (1953) *Asia and Western Domination*. London: Allen and
Unwin.

Parry, J.H. (1974) *Trade and Dominion*. London: Cardinal.

Pratt, M.L. (1992) *Imperial Eyes: Travel Writing and Transculturation*.
London: Routledge.

Richardson, M. (1990) 'Enough Said – Reflections of Orientalism', *Anthro-*
pology Today, 6 (4): 16–19.

Said, E. (1978) *Orientalism*. London: Routledge and Kegan Paul.

Said, E. (1983) *The World, the Text and the Critic*. Harvard: Harvard University Press.

Said, E. (1993) *Culture and Imperialism*. London: Chatto and Windus.

Said, E. (1994) *Representations of the Intellectual*. London: Vintage.

Said, E. (1994) *The Politics of Dispossession*. New York: Pantheon Books.

Sardar, Z. (1992) 'When Dracula Meets the "Other": Europe, Columbus and the Columbian Legacy', *Alternatives*, 17: 493–517.

Sardar, Z. (1996/7) 'Walt Disney and the Double Victimisation of Pocahontas', *Third Text*, 37: 17–27.

Sardar, Z. (1998) *Postmodernism and the Other*, London: Pluto Press.

Sardar, Z. (1999) 'Development and the location of eurocentrism' in R. Munck and D. O'Hearn (eds) *Critical Development Theory: Contributions to a New Paradigm*. Zed Books, London.

Sardar, Z. and Davies, M.W. (1990) *Distorted Imagination: Lessons from the Rushdie Affair*. London: Grey Seal.

Sardar, Z., Davies, M.W. and Nandy, A. (1993), *Barbaric Others: A Manifesto on Western Racism*. London: Pluto Press.

Shaheen, J. (1985) *The TV Arab*. Bowling Green, Ohio: Bowling Green State University Popular Culture Press.

Shaheen, J. (1987) 'The Hollywood Arab', *Journal of Popular Film and Television*, 14 (4): 148–57.

Sharpe, J. (1993) *Allegories of Empire: The Figure of Woman in the Colonial Text*. Minneapolis: University of Minnesota Press.

Shohat, E. and Stam, R. (1994) *Unthinking Eurocentrism: Multiculturalism and the Media*. London: Routledge.

Singer, M.R. (1964) *The Emerging Elite*. Cambridge, Massachusetts: MIT Press.

Soguk, N. (1993) 'Reflections on the 'Orientalised Orientals', *Alternatives*, 18: 361–38.

Southern, R.W. (1962) *Western Views of Islam in the Middle Ages*. Cambridge, Massachusetts: Harvard.

Southern, R.W. (1970) *Western Society and the Church in the Middle Ages*. Harmondsworth: Penguin.

Spence, J. (1998) *The Great Chan's Great Continent: China in Western Minds*. New York: W.W. Norton.

Sprinker, M. (1992) *Edward Said: A Critical Reader*. Oxford: Blackwell.

Spurr, D. (1993) *The Rhetoric of Empire: Colonial Discourse in Journalism, Travel Writing, and Imperial Administration*. Durham: Duke University Press.

Suleri, S. (1992) *The Rhetoric of English India*. Chicago: The University of Chicago Press.

Thapar, R. (1992) *Interpreting Early India*. Delhi: Oxford University Press.

Tibawi, A.L. (1964) *English Speaking Orientalists*. London: Luzac.

Tibawi, A.L. (1976) *Arabic and Islamic Themes*. London: Luzac.

Turner, B.S. (1994) *Orientalism, Postmodernism & Globalism*. London: Routledge.

Ueno, T. (1997) 'Japanimation and Techno-Orientalism' in M.B. Roetto (ed.) *ISEA 96 Proceedings: Seventh International Symposium on Electronic Art*. Rotterdam: ISEA 96 Foundation.

Vittachi, V.T. (1987) *The Brown Sahib Revisited*. Delhi: Penguin.

Waardenburg, J. (1963) *L'Islam dans le miroir de l'Occident*. The Hague: Mouton.

Williams, G.A. (1996) *Excalibur*. London: BBC.

Wittfogel, K. (1981) *Oriental Despotism: A Study in Total Power*. New York: Vintage Books.

Young, R. (1990) *White Mythologies: Writing History and the West*. London: Routledge.

Index

Index